BRUCE CHATWIN

For Sue

BRUCE CHATWIN

Nicholas Murray

Border Lines Series Editor
John Powell Ward

SEREN BOOKS

SEREN BOOKS is the book imprint of
Poetry Wales Press Ltd
Andmar House, Tondu Road, Bridgend, Mid Glamorgan

© Nicholas Murray, 1993

Second Impression, 1993

British Library Cataloguing in Publication Data

Murray, Nicholas
Bruce Chatwin. — (Border Lines Series)
I. Title II. Series
823.914

ISBN 1-85411-079-9
1-85411-080-2 paperback

The publisher acknowledges the financial support of the
Welsh Arts Council

Printed in Palatino
by The Cromwell Press, Broughton Gifford

CONTENTS

List of Illustrations

I myself have been tempted for a long time by the cloud-moving wind — filled with a strong desire to wander

Matsuo Basho (1644-94)

1. Approaching Chatwin

There is only one school of writing," announced Vladimir Nabokov, "that of talent." Bruce Chatwin, one of the most original and interesting writers to have emerged in Britain in the 1970s and 1980s, is a writer who defies easy classification. He appears to belong to no group or tendency, and to be entirely resistant to neat critical placing. Even as a travel writer, the most tempting designation, he differs so greatly from his peers that the term seems to offer little illumination. That he was a graduate of the school of talent, however, is beyond dispute.

In the Welsh border country he is known, pre-eminently, as the author of *On The Black Hill*, a book which established itself almost immediately as a classic fictional depiction of the life of the Radnorshire hill-farming community (although it was always much more than this). Apparently without effort, it joined the company of Kilvert's *Diary* and the novels of Mary Webb, as an essential key to the literary interpretation of the area to itself. If it is legitimate to talk of a literature of the Welsh borders then *On The Black Hill* is one of its canonical texts. And all this happened in less than a decade.

Yet in spite of the specificity of the novel's portrait of Radnorshire life — its author was deservedly dubbed "the demon-researcher" by John Updike — its interpretation would be partial and inadequate without an appreciation of the rest of Chatwin's work and of the ideas that run through and around all his writing. This chronicle of the lives of two identical twins on an upland Radnorshire sheep farm — which is also the chronicle of a century that sometimes seemed to run past The Vision farmhouse like a river identified only by the sound of its rushing water — came from the pen of a writer who had previously depicted the isolated, apparently marginalised lives of the more unusual inhabitants of the southern tip of the South American continent in Patagonia. He had recounted the life of an exiled Brazilian slave trader in the barbarous kingdom of Dahomey on the slave coast of West Africa and would go on to explore the territory and myth of the central Australian desert. His final novel was the story of an obsessive Czech collector of Meissen porcelain which turned into a parable about the meaning and purpose of art.

It is vital, in short, to grasp the place of On The Black Hill on the author's peculiar and highly original intellectual map. The diversity of Bruce Chatwin's books — each one seeming to spring from an entirely different source and to confound the expectation raised by its predecessor — should not prevent us from recognising the deep continuities between each of them and the way in which they were always the reflection of a brilliant and idiosyncratic inquiring mind that continually revisited a certain set of obsessive ideas about that original restlessness in human nature which he himself so strikingly embodied.

Thus, when Amos Jones descends into the market town of Rhulen on the day of festivities to celebrate the relief of Mafeking on 18 May 1899, after a bitter winter in which he has quarrelled with his wife and "rushed out into the dark" to wander and sleep rough, he reconciles himself to her by saying: "Be the winter as makes me mad." When we know of Chatwin's theories about the innate restlessness of human beings, of "the sins of settlement", of the speculation that we are a naturally migratory species damagingly incarcerated in the prison compounds of civilisation (ideas which are expounded most fully in The Songlines), we see Amos Jones's words in a new light. His anguish, in Chatwin's scheme, is the anguish of a man whose natural need to make a seasonal migration is suppressed by the requirement that he anchor himself to the implacable demands of the hill farm in winter.

Bruce Chatwin claimed The Songlines as "a novel of ideas". He had little interest in the contemporary English novel and what he saw as its comparatively narrow range of concerns. He liked to paint on a bigger, more exhilarating thematic canvas even if his method in books such as Utz might seem, paradoxically, to be that of the miniaturist. His unashamed passion for ideas can be seen as an aspect of his flight — Chatwin was an accomplished escapologist — from a certain idea of Englishness.

In the autumn of 1974, as Chatwin quit his job as a freelance journalist with *The Sunday Times Magazine* and headed for Patagonia to start to research his first book, the cosmopolitan critic George Steiner wrote in the *Times Literary Supplement*:

> For motives too complex, too serious to be casually enumerated, the climate of British feeling over recent decades has favoured ironic constraint, sparsity of idiom and shape. The normative posture is one of wary thrift or ironic deflation, in respect of style, theme, personal investment. The grand notion, the "copious", to borrow a term used by Donald Davie, are distrusted. (Steiner, 1975)

The poet Ezra Pound had made the same point with rather more economy half a century earlier:

> England has always loved the man incapable of thought... (Pound, 1916)

Chatwin's "normative posture" was to ask the big questions and to write books which dealt with what one critic called the "dirty great issues of life and death". At a time when English novelists mostly stayed at home Chatwin travelled the world — in pursuit of knowledge as much as "material" — feeding his intellectual obsessions, risking bolder and bolder speculations. And he took his readers with him. His most intellectually ambitious book, *The Songlines*, was also his most successful commercially, a late best-seller whose financial success surprised and reportedly pleased him. Yet as much as a quarter of the book was made up of extracts from his notebooks containing quotations arranged in a carefully suggestive pattern to illustrate aspects of his passionate interest in the desert nomads in particular and what he identified as his "question of questions, the nature of human restlessness" in general. Perhaps some readers (unwisely) skimmed these passages but it was nonetheless a testimony to Chatwin's unusual gifts as a writer that he could pull off a feat that in other hands might have ended horribly as a parade of *longeurs*.

Chatwin's books are so original that they defy easy categorisation. To the eternal confusion of librarians and booksellers his books straddle the genres of novel and travel-writing and blur the distinction between fact and fiction. His second novel won the Whitbread Award for Best First Novel and no one could quite decide what *The Songlines* was, after Chatwin won an argument with his publisher to call it a novel. His own preferred term for their mix of fact, fiction, autobiography, anthropology, travel reportage and boundless intellectual inquiry, was "searches". Like a contemporary intellectual knight errant he pursued the holy grail of a key to understanding the source of the human inclination to wander. It was a modern version of the literature of quest.

It was one of Bruce Chatwin's achievements to have breathed new life into the literature of travel, yet he and his admirers hated the term 'travel writer'. Although part of the mid-1980s boom in travel writing and publishing, he maintained his own distinctively personal style. Where some travel writers can give the impression of travelling simply in order to find the material for a book, before moving on to the next commission, Chatwin travelled with a genuine passion to inquire. He showed no anxiety about wasting material, doing so with a marvellous prodigality. The list of places he visited but did not write about far exceeds those he did succeed in getting on to paper.

Chatwin was also a highly accomplished prose stylist. His spare, swift, economical prose is a rebuke to the prolixity and purple that have so often trammelled the travel writing genre. He was incapable of writing a slipshod or uninteresting sentence and the relative brevity of his books was the necessary outcome of an art that did not waste itself. Even the most apparently slight of his books carried considerable weight. His writing was vivid, direct and informed by a vital enthusiasm and infectious energy. There was nothing cynical or pessimistic or disillusioned in Chatwin's outlook, which makes reading him always an exhilarating experience. Here he is in a characteristic passage from *In Patagonia*, describing an evening meal at the hotel at Port Madryn in Welsh Patagonia:

> At dinner the waiter wore white gloves and served a lump of burnt lamb that bounced on the plate. Spread over the restaurant wall was an immense canvas of gauchos herding cattle into an orange

sunset. An old-fashioned blonde gave up on the lamb and sat painting her nails. An Indian came in drunk and drank through three jugs of wine. His eyes were glittering slits in the red leather shield of his face. The jugs were of green plastic in the shape of penguins.(*In Patagonia*, p.24)

Many accounts exist of Bruce Chatwin's captivating presence. He was strikingly handsome with piercing blue eyes, and possessed a reportedly spellbinding gift for telling stories, which combined with a relentless intellectual energy. He was an omnivorous reader and a brilliant talker. Until his final illness began to leave its mark on him he maintained a permanently youthful air. The travel-writer Patrick Leigh Fermor, at whose home on the steep coast of the Peloponnese Chatwin stayed while writing parts of *The Songlines*, recalls his "buoyant alertness, the effulgent eyes, the high forehead under tousled fair hair — like that of some schoolboys, it refused to lie flat on the crown". Chatwin, he felt, "had the utterly convincing aura of an infant prodigy".

Chatwin's friend Salman Rushdie, who accompanied Chatwin on his travels in the Australian desert and who may have been a partial model for Arkady in *The Songlines*, was one of many who left descriptions of Chatwin that seem to be laying the foundations of a legend:

> He was a magnificent raconteur of Scheherazadean inexhaustibility, a gilt-edged name-dropper, a voracious reader of esoteric texts, a scholar gipsy, a mimic — his Mrs Ghandi was perfect — and a giggler of international class. He was as talkative as he was curious, and he was curious about everything... His words about the ex-Chamberlain of King Zog of Albania are truer of himself: 'People of his kind will never come again. What a voice we lost when his fell silent! How much he still had to say'. (Rushdie, 1991, p.237)

Chatwin's conversational brilliance, however, is more often asserted than demonstrated. So far, at any rate, he has lacked his Boswell, and, like the dance that Isadora Duncan danced, we must take these descriptions on trust and leave the rest to imagination, or await future accounts.

Some of Bruce Chatwin's friends record that he was paradoxically reticent, in the midst of his extreme sociability, and frequently presented himself to them as an enigma. Writing about his posthumous collection of collected writings, *What Am I Doing Here*, Salman Rushdie observed in 1989:

> In this book, as in his life, Bruce Chatwin is secretive about the workings of his heart. I wish it were not so, for he was a man of great heart and deep feeling, but he rarely let it into his prose. (Rushdie, 1991, p.239)

The novelist and travel writer Colin Thubron — another friend and admirer (though he held some reservations about *The Song-lines*) observed: "In private he is compulsively articulate, yet he projects a public enigma." And another friend, Michael Ignatieff, in an important interview with Chatwin in the magazine *Granta* in 1987 followed a sketch of his interviewee ("An indefatigable fabulist and story teller...a lapidary talker...") with the observation that Chatwin was "English in his use of self-deprecation as a strategy of disguise." For Ignatieff, Chatwin's outward identity as a thoroughly orthodox middle class Englishman was one "he has spent a lifetime escaping".

Chatwin once admitted that his instinct when things got difficult was to run away and he seems to have spent the whole course of his life on the move. This tempts us to enquire: what was he running from? Was his intellectual inquiry into human restlessness an objective investigation or a *post hoc* rationalisation of his own unease? Until we know more about Bruce Chatwin's life such questions must, inevitably, be deferred.

Certainly, he was drawn to people at the margins, eccentrics "away from the centre", out of the apparent mainstream. Part of the irresistible fascination of the Welsh border country was the sense that in this distinctive territory between England and Wales people were different, in ways that seemed to resist the insistent contemporary pressures of conformity and material consumption that he was increasingly to criticise. Accused of writing about the eccentric and the bizarre, he argued that the people he observed, in Patagonia or Radnorshire, for example, were perhaps closer to the centre of things. "When you start to examine so-called eccentric characters," he told Melvyn Bragg in a television interview, "you find that they're extremely sane and they're not particularly eccentric — they're just living on a

different time scale, in a different world." Although he recorded
the changes forced by history on the lifestyle of his Radnorshire
farmers — and it is not always recognised, particularly by the
literary people who made the novel something of a cult book in
the 1980s, that the book was far from being a comfortable ideali-
sation of Welsh rural life — he speculated after *On The Black Hill*
was written that some of the traditional ways might survive.
The young people who inherited the farm, whose flashy mod-
ernity was foregrounded in their representation in the novel,
might end up, he thought, by establishing a new connection
with its traditions.

In this he showed himself to be something of a conservative.
Although he was open to newness in the visual arts and wrote
interestingly about such avant-garde movements as Russian Futurism, he had little time for literary experiment. " I'm unimpressed by the idea of the new. Most advances in literature
usually strike me as being advances into a cul-de-sac," he told
an interviewer.

More importantly perhaps, his thought was concerned with
the recovery of certain things which he believed the modern
world had neglected. It was, in that sense, backward looking.
He was a constant critic of contemporary Western materialism
and an advocate of a new asceticism (who had to accept the
counter-charge that there was little Franciscan poverty in his
own material circumstances). This austerity he saw, like the
contemporary Green movements, as a necessary strategy for
survival. He was repeatedly to declare: "If the world has a future, it is an ascetic future."

This study of Bruce Chatwin is concerned primarily with the
writing and the ideas that informed it. But he was a frequently
autobiographical writer who would not have understood the
critical formality of separating the life from the work. A major
authorised biography of Chatwin has been commissioned and
is likely to appear in three or four years' time. Through access to
material as yet unavailable this biography may provide answers
to the questions that readers of Chatwin are currently lacking
and it is eagerly awaited. The present study however also
draws widely on printed and broadcast sources together with
further original research to provide what it is hoped is a useful
introductory account of Bruce Chatwin's life and work. The

writer's final illness has been the object of much comment and speculation — discussed in chapter seven below — but, given our current state of knowledge, any attempt to use it speculatively as the basis for critical judgements has been avoided.

2. BEFORE PATAGONIA

Charles Bruce Chatwin was born in wartime Sheffield on 13 May 1940. His father, Charles, a Birmingham lawyer in civilian life, was in the Royal Navy, serving on a mine-sweeper in Cardiff Bay. Bruce and his mother, Margharita, spent much of the War in a nomadic drift from one set of dismal, temporary lodgings to another. It was a time when, as he told an interviewer: "I lived in NAAFI canteens and was passed around like a tea urn". He was later to write, with perhaps a shade of fellow-feeling, that the writer Sybille Bedford appeared to have been " born on the move". These early childhood experiences point, inescapably, to his later obsessions.

The man who was to write one of the best known modern novels about Wales had his family roots deep in the heart of middle class, middle England. He came from a line of what he termed " Birmingham worthies" and " solid sedentary citizens": sturdy professional people from the Midlands, architects and lawyers who could trace themselves back to a Birmingham button maker. In a valuable autobiographical essay published in the *New York Times* in 1983, he referred to a number of slightly less " worthy" forebears, " legendary figures whose histories inflamed my imagination". The essay introduces a cast of characters that shows Chatwin at work trying to construct, perhaps, a more raffish pedigree than his immediate background would appear to warrant. Great-great-grandfather Mathieson, for instance, who at the age of seventy-one won the tossing of the caber at the Highland Games "and died promptly of a stroke" or great-grandfather Milward who was " a man obsessed by money" and the friend of Gounod and Adelina Patti. One afternoon Bruce was rummaging through an old tin trunk and found his great grandfather's court suit and marcasite-handled sword:

> Dressed as a courtier, sword in hand, I dashed into the drawing room shouting, "Look what I've found!" — and was told to "take those things off at once!" Poor Great-grandpapa! His name was taboo. Convicted for fraud in 1902, he was allowed out of prison to die. (Chatwin, 1983)

There was also "Cousin Charley Milward the Sailor", whose part in engendering *In Patagonia* will be recorded later, and Uncle Geoffrey, an Arabist and desert traveller who, with a smack of T.E. Lawrence, was given a golden headdress by the Emir Feisal and who "died poor in Cairo". The final pair were Uncle Bickerton "pick miner and bigamist" and Uncle Humphrey, whose obituary is brief even by Chatwin's standards: " Sad end in Africa."

Having lugged these skeletons enthusiastically out of the closet, Chatwin goes on to observe that the etymology of 'Chatwin' could have been the Anglo-Saxon " chette-wynde" or " winding path" and notes in passing a dynasty of Mormon Chatwins in a remote part of Utah. He also claims to have heard of " a Mr and Mrs Chatwin, trapeze artists" .

In the second chapter of *The Songlines*, Chatwin underlines the connection between his childhood portability and his attraction to the nomads by recalling a childhood picture of an Aboriginal family on the move with whom he identified. He goes on:

> I remember the fantastic homelessness of my first five years. My father was in the Navy, at sea. My mother and I would shuttle back and forth, on the railways of wartime England, on visits to family and friends.
>
> All the frenzied agitation of that time communicated itself to me: this hiss of steam on a fogbound station; the double *clu-unk* of carriage doors closing; the drone of the aircraft, the searchlights, the sirens; the sound of a mouth-organ along a platform of sleeping soldiers. (*The Songlines*, p.7)

For a writer normally so faithful to the Nabokovian precept of " no delight without the detail" there is an untypical air of cliché about this picture of wartime railway stations and wafting harmonicas that perhaps suggests some nostalgic retouching. But the dislocations and constant movement were real enough for the small boy.

His earliest childhood recollection was of staying with his maternal grandmother Turnell in furnished rooms on the seafront at Filey in Yorkshire where he watched the grey convoys passing to and fro across the horizon. He waved at the ships as they vanished behind Flamborough Head, the possible starting point for his admired Rimbaud's prose poem 'Promontoire'. At dusk his Aberdonian grandmother would draw the blackout curtains, turn on the bakelite wireless, and everyone would listen to the BBC news. To celebrate the Battle of Alamein his mother and grandmother danced the Highland fling around the room, leaving the boy to take his grandmother's stockings as a dancing partner. Sam Turnell was "a sad-eyed solitary whose only real accomplishment was an impeccable tap dance". Chatwin said that he worshipped Sam (who became a salesman of memorial glass windows after the Battle of Britain) and, when the Chatwins temporarily rented a disused shop in Derbyshire, Bruce acquired from him a love of long walks over the moors.

It was at Filey that his love of books began, although: "The usual run of children's books left me cold." The first grown up book he read from cover to cover was Joshua Slocum's *Sailing Alone Around the World*. On his third birthday, his father took him bicycling on Flamborough Head, an excursion described in one of the brief but vivid prose pieces he wrote in the last year of his life. Like his son, Charles Chatwin had striking blue eyes:

> My father has the most beautiful blue eyes I have ever seen in a man. I do not say this because he is my father. They are mariner's eyes, level and steady. On the Malta convoys they scanned the surface of the sea for mines, or the horizon for an enemy warship. They are the eyes of a man who has never known the meaning of dishonesty. They have never tempted him to anything mean or shoddy. (*What Am I Doing Here*, p.9)

This is a rare moment in Chatwin's writing, where he is showing us his heart. But even here there is a stiff and filial rectitude about the portrait. In this piece, Chatwin also describes his mother's eyes as being "brown and lively, with suggestions of Southern ancestry". In an interview with Colin Thubron he noted the colour of his grandmother's eyes, too, ("flinty green") and suggests that she had something of the gipsy about her.

One of his earliest memories, he tells Thubron, was of being on the Yorkshire moors and his grandmother shouting to his mother a warning that the gipsies might take young Bruce. Then he saw, just over the hedge, a whole line of caravans moving up a lane, and a gipsy boy, stripped to the waist and very brown, riding by on a piebald pony. Bruce thought: "My life isn't as it should be."

At the age of four, Bruce went to stay with his great aunts Janie and Gracie in their terraced house behind the church at Stratford-upon-Avon. This episode appears in the second chapter of *The Songlines* where their names are changed to Great Aunts Katie and Ruth. Bruce set himself up as a guide to the Shakespeare monuments and tomb at threepence a go. Most of his customers were American GIs. Great Aunt Gracie/Ruth had travelled only once in her life to Flanders to lay a wreath on a loved one's grave. But from the way she talked of the " horizon struck wanderers" in the Chatwin family tree, Bruce suspected her of feeling the trouble of the " wanderer in her soul". She was very deaf and carried a deaf aid the size of a portable radio. On Fridays she took young Bruce to the parish church with her to clean it and deck the altar with flowers while he clambered into the pulpit " or held imaginary conversations with Mr Shakespeare"The first lines of verse he learned by heart were the four lines on the Bard's tomb:

> Good frend, for Jesus sake, forbeare
> To digge the dust encloased here
> Bleste be ye man yt spares thes stones
> And curst be he yt moves my bones.

Many years later, in Hungary, he recalled these lines at an excavation. Some peasant women in the fields had cried out to the archaeologists opening a Hunnish princess's grave to leave her with her lover, Zeus. " I began to wonder if archaeology itself were not cursed," he mused. On summer days Great Aunt Gracie would take Bruce, with her cocker spaniel Amber, to the bank of the Avon at a place called Weir Brake which she insisted (although Chatwin was later to decide that it was more suitable as Ophelia's drowning place) was the bank whereon the wild thyme blew. She read him poetry from an anthology

called *The Open Road* which had a green buckram binding and a
flight of gilded swallows on the cover. He had a thorough
grounding in the conventional anthology pieces and discovered
" the strident, beckoning music of Walt Whitman". His favourite bedtime reading was Ernest Thompson Seton's *Lives of
the Hunted*, about a coyote pup who escaped to the wild. As he
got a little older he took advantage of the proximity of the
Shakespeare theatre by cycling through the dawn to make sure
of getting one of the unreserved seats at the back row of the
stalls. He saw most of the great productions of the late 1940s
and 1950s, with Olivier, Gielgud, Peggy Ashcroft and Paul
Robeson as Othello which he said "constitute for me the Shakespeare of all time. Having lived the plays as a boy, I can now
scarcely sit through one without a sensation of loss."

Great Aunt Janie/Katie was a painter and had travelled. The
" elder and wittier" of the two old maids, she had attended
Bohemian parties in Paris, and had been a nurse in the Great
War. " Perhaps," Chatwin speculated, " the deaths of so many
beautiful youths moved her to paint the canvasses of St Sebastian that lay in racks around her studio". Great Aunt Janie was
" a tireless reader of modern fiction" and would later tell Bruce
that "Americans wrote better, cleaner English than the English
themselves". It was from her that he first heard the name of
Ernest Hemingway, his acknowledged mentor in prose style.
One day she looked up from her novel and declared: " What a
wonderful word 'arse' is!"

Eventually, towards the end of the war, the Chatwins moved
back to their "grim-gabled" house in the Birmingham suburbs
where Charles Chatwin would later resume his career as a lawyer, coming home exhausted in the evenings after "grappling
with the problems of National Health Service Hospitals". At
first Bruce grew sick and thin and in " the heady months before
the Normandy landings" people wondered if he was going to
become tubercular. Chatwin's own diagnosis, unlikely to have
been endorsed by the average Brummagem G.P., was that he
was suffering from Baudelaire's *"grande maladie: horreur du domicile"*. When his mother rushed upstairs one morning with
news of the surrender of Japan: " I glanced at the photo of the
mushroom cloud and knew something dreadful had happened.
The curtains of my bedroom were woven with tongues of

orange flame. That night, and for years to come, I dreamed of walking over a charred black landscape with my hair on fire." The image of The Bomb recurs throughout Chatwin's writing and its terrifying possibilities continued to haunt him.

By 1949 the Chatwins had resumed a settled bourgeois prosperity and one evening Charles Chatwin came home from work in a new car. It was a Lanchester which had been sitting in Bruce's great uncle's barn since before the war. The next day his father took him and his brother Hugh for a spin. On the edge of an escarpment, Charles Chatwin stopped and pointed to a range of grey hills in the West and announced that they were going to press on into Wales. They crossed the border and parked the car in a field in Radnorshire. They woke the next morning to a heavy dew and found they were surrounded by a circle of ruminative sheep. The seed of *On The Black Hill* had been planted.

On Guy Fawkes day in the same year the masters at Bruce's prep school encouraged the boys to burn on a bonfire an effigy of the Labour Prime Minister Clement Atlee. " I was sad for Mr Atlee," wrote Chatwin, " and never, even in my capitalist phase, was I able to vote Conservative." He professed himself unable to understand the mysteries of the English class system — although it could have presented few difficulties for him — yet *On The Black Hill* shows a perfectly competent grasp of its working out. The *Daily Telegraph*, in a characteristic formulation, was later to call him: "A snobbish democrat who voted Socialist". But he was not a political rebel and claimed rather to have been " ostracized for telling tall stories" and, more pertinently, to have become " an addict of atlases". He started at school his lifetime habit of reading voraciously — John C. Voss's *The Venturesome Voyages of Captain Voss*, Melville's *Omoo* and *Typee*, then Richard Henry Dana and Jack London. "Perhaps from these writers I got a taste for Yankee plain style?" he speculated. He never liked Jules Verne, believing that "the real was always more fantastic than the fantastical".

Bruce Chatwin was a war baby but a Cold War schoolboy. The global terrors of nuclear war, whipped up by civil defence lecturers in khaki shorts with " white and knobbly" knees, woke in him "a passion for geography" (*In Patagonia*, p.6) and: "In the late 1940s the Cannibal of the Kremlin shadowed our lives; you could mistake his moustaches for teeth." At school the boys started an Emigration Committee and made plans to settle in some far corner of the earth. Poring over atlases they fixed eventually on Patagonia as the safest place on earth. But then, in 1953, Stalin died and the boys sang hymns of praise in chapel: "but I continued to hold Patagonia in reserve".

That same year Bruce was sent to Sweden for the summer to talk English to a boy of his age with whom, it turned out, he had little in common. But the boy's Uncle Percival was "a delightful old gentleman, always dressed in white smock and sun hat". Bruce would walk with him through the birch forest, gather mushrooms or row to an island to see the nesting ospreys. Uncle Percival lived in a log cabin lit by crystal chandeliers and had travelled in Czarist Russia. He made Bruce read Chekhov in Constance Garnett's translation and also Duff Cooper's biography of Talleyrand. The great English novelists, he says, were left unread, although in later adolescence, when he was sent to the Birmingham Eye Hospital with partial paralysis of the optic nerve, he listened to *Oliver Twist, Wuthering Heights* and *Pride and Prejudice* on gramophone records "in plummy English voices".

After prep school Chatwin went to Marlborough College where he says he was considered "a dimwit and a dreamer". That is not the recollection of his schoolfriend and room-mate at Marlborough, Michael Cannon, who remembers Bruce as a popular boy whose legendary talents for storytelling and mimicry were already well developed. Cannon knew the family, too, as Birmingham neighbours, and describes them as having "a very ordinary sort of middle class background, tastes and attitudes". He adds: "Bruce produced this enormous talent from where I just don't really know." Bruce was not as obsessed as others by rugger and hockey and was "more an artistic sort of chap" who acted in school plays and went up the classics side of Marlborough. He claimed that he was always "bottom of the class" in classics, which Cannon doubts, and was taught classics by Alan Whitehorn, father of the *Observer* journalist Katherine Whitehorn.

While his friends were on the playing field Bruce was off on his bicycle exploring the surrounding Wiltshire countryside, visiting churches — and antique shops. He was a precocious collector and would return balancing prodigious piles of antiques on his crossbar. His later friend and travelling companion, the poet and scholar Peter Levi, says that Bruce made large sums of money at Marlborough by buying from one antique dealer and selling to another "until all the local dealers in a body came and protested to the headmaster". The results of his acquisitions were on display in the study bedroom he shared with Michael Cannon — a fabulous decor of white and pastel lime wallpaper stocked with minor Italian masters and antique English furniture. "Our study was probably the best furnished study Marlborough has ever had," recalls Michael Cannon. Porters showing prospective parents around would sometimes knock on the door and ask if their parties might be allowed a glimpse of the legendary interior.

The two boys once went on an illicit bicycle ride through the moonlit Wiltshire lanes, pedalling briskly on unlit machines, to see the sun rise at Stonehenge at the summer solstice. But mostly Bruce seems to have kept his own company. According to Michael Cannon he was considered mildly eccentric ("but Marlborough always had a certain number of people who were like that") and stood apart by a certain independence and maturity (in spite of his legendary boyish appearance) which made him more interesting, thinks Cannon, to some of the masters who appreciated his originality: "He had perhaps a bit more dignity than the rest of us, rushing around the rugger field and so on." He was also an entertainer who would put on a silk dressing gown and sing the Noel Coward songs at the piano which he had first learned to sing to the wind-up gramophone. His mimicry was perfect: "You could close your eyes and it *was* Noel Coward."

Much later, in the early 1970s, Bruce met Noel Coward at a lunch party hosted in London by Anne Fleming, widow of Ian, before The Master "crept off to die in Jamaica". Lady Diana Cooper was also present, with Merle Oberon. Chatwin had told the story of that occasion many times to friends but eventually, in one of those short pieces written in his last months during 1988, he finally set it on paper:

On the way out from lunch he said, "I have very much enjoyed meeting you, but unfortunately, we will never meet again because very shortly I will be dead. *But* if you'll take one parting word of advice, "Never let anything artistic stand in your way." (*What am I Doing Here*, p.36)

Chatwin claimed that he always acted on this advice. His readers have been the beneficiaries of the fact that he did no such thing.

It would have been normal for Bruce to have done the Marlborough thing and gone straight to one of the ancient universities. He was bright and well read and a keen exploiter of the outstanding school library. In addition he had patronised the town bookshop so well that on his seventeenth birthday its owner gave him a copy of Edith Sitwell's anthology *Planet and Glowworm*, "a collection of texts for insomniacs". Chatwin traced a number of enduring literary obsessions and influences to these selections: Baudelaire, Nerval and Rimbaud, Li Po and other Chinese " wanderers", Blake and Christopher Smart, John Aubrey's brief lives, and " the seventeenth century prose music of Jeremy Taylor" — who would provide the epigraph to *On The Black Hill* — and Sir Thomas Browne. At the age of fifteen he acquired a copy of a classic 1930s travel book, *The Road to Oxiana* by Robert Byron, which he raised to the status of a sacred text and which "spineless and floodstained after four journeys to Central Asia" (*What Am I Doing Here*, p.287) he carried with him for the rest of his life. He sought out Byron's friends and pestered them for their reminiscences, although he would be twenty-two before he actually set off in Byron's footsteps. The idea of becoming a writer had still not entered his head and he would in fact be thirty-seven before his first book was published. But what was he to do next?

He told his schoolfriends briskly that they were all very " boring" going off to university. Talked out of a career on the stage by his family, he also rejected the traditional family profession of architecture because he considered himself innumerate and therefore incapable of passing the necessary examinations. Deciding that his talents were so obviously visual he started work, in December 1958, as a uniformed porter at the London fine art auctioneers, Sotheby and Co of Bond Street. His wages were six pounds a week.

Bruce Chatwin's first job at Sotheby's was in the ceramics department, numbering pieces of porcelain ready for sale. Modest though this start in life was, his schoolfriends were impressed. Michael Cannon, by now an undergraduate at Cambridge, found it very exciting that he had a friend who actually had a flat in London — a tiny place in Grosvenor Crescent Mews at the back of St George's Hospital — where he could come and stay. On a return visit to Cambridge, Chatwin stalked through the corridors of the Fitzwilliam Museum announcing "Fake!" "Genuine!" "Fake!" as he surveyed the picture galleries. He had what is known in the fine arts as " the eye" and it was not long in coming to the attention of his superiors.

He spent barely six months labelling pots, then moved briefly into the furniture department before finding his permanent home in the Impressionist and Antiquities department where he was joined by Michel Strauss. At about this time, and certainly very early in his career, an incident occurred which has figured repeatedly in profiles and obituary notices but which appears to have slipped the corporate memory of Sotheby's who were unable to confirm it. Chatwin, in his grey porter's overall, is said to have spotted a Picasso gouache of a harlequin and promptly declared it a fake. But Michel Strauss, who still works at Sotheby's, is sceptical of this story, observing drily: "We are spotting fake Picassos all the time here."

An alternative version, from Michael Cannon, is that his ability to read the inscriptions on Greek amphorae drew his employers' attention to his true abilities. Whatever the truth — and Chatwin's habit of vividly enhancing the literal narrative makes verification far from easy — it was clear that Chatwin's gifts had been recognised by the firm and his meteoric rise from schoolboy porter to the youngest ever director of the firm had begun.

Chatwin was later to disparage both his earlier self and the art world in which it shone. Auctions and art dealers were always portrayed unflatteringly in his books. Nevertheless, he spent eight years at Sotheby's, and met some fascinating people. He travelled widely in his work, too, before discovering how "smarmy", in his own words, he had become. "I was an instant expert," he wrote, "flying here and there to pronounce, with unbelievable arrogance, on the value or authenticity of works of art. I particularly enjoyed telling people that their paintings were fake." His boyish demeanour persisted: a woman on Park Avenue in New York slammed the door in his face, shouting " I'm not showing my Renoir to a 16-year-old kid!"

The high points of his career he considered to be a conversation with Andre Breton about the fruit machines in Reno; the discovery of a Tahiti Gaugin in a crumbling Scottish castle; and an afternoon with Georges Braque "who, in a white leather jacket, a white tweed cap and a lilac chiffon scarf, allowed me to sit in his studio while he painted a flying bird". He met Picasso and Giacometti and established a network of contacts across the globe while still in his early twenties. Peter Levi met him when he was at Sotheby's and recalled that "his jokes tended to refer to what Picasso had said to him last week about Tony Armstrong Jones". He was successful and reasonably off in what was known as Swinging London in the early sixties and is said to have attended a party in 1964 at the nightclub Regine wearing a live python as a bow tie. He now lived in a flat " behind Hyde Park Corner" which his friend the painter Howard Hodgkin described as having "the most dandyish interior I had ever seen". Chatwin had recently come back from a recuperative desert journey in the Sudan when Hodgkin called (his explorations and travels began in his periods of leave from Sotheby's) and had given the flat's sitting room "a monochromatic desert-like atmosphere". He adorned it with two works of art only, " the arse of an archaic Greek marble *kouros*, and an early seventeenth century Japanese screen". Hodgkin came for a dinner party and, as a result, the interior passed into his painting *The Japanese Screen*. Chatwin considered that he was "the acid green smear on the left" in this picture. In a hopeful interpretation he also saw the green smear " turning away in disgust, away from my guests, away from my possessions, away from the 'dandified' interior, and possibly back to the Sahara" (*What Am I Doing Here*, p.76). The end of his career in the art world was approaching.

It is perhaps unsurprising that Chatwin, now the youthful head — at the age of twenty-five — of Sotheby's Impressionist Department and soon to be one of its youngest ever partners, managed to catch the attention of the gossip columnists. On 12 July 1965 a brief item appeared in the London *Evening Standard* headed 'Love among the pictures'. It began:

A romance which had been bubbling behind the scenes in the Impressionist picture department at Sotheby's came to a head today when Mr Bruce Chatwin, the 25-year old head of the department, announced his engagement to Miss Elizabeth Chanler, the American secretary of Mr Peter Wilson, Sotheby's chairman.

The wedding took place in August. Elizabeth, aged twenty-six, and educated at Radcliffe, was the daughter of a retired U.S. admiral who had been at Pearl Harbor. Chatwin later wrote that when he heard her tell a story he decided "this was a woman I could marry". They shared a love of travel and she often accompanied him on trips. When Chatwin lay ill in the Radcliffe Infirmary at Oxford in the last year of his life, Elizabeth would, according to Roger Clarke, who collaborated with Chatwin on a projected opera based on the work of Rimbaud, bring him her own shepherd's pies as an alternative to hospital food. He told Clarke proudly: "Elizabeth is a shepherdess. It's on her passport", and for many years they lived in rural Gloucestershire at Wotton under Edge. They lived later in a beautiful house in Oxfordshire described by Michael Ignatieff as "a raspberry red clapboard farmhouse, which belongs on a Vermont hillside but is actually on the edge of sloping pastures in the Chilterns near Oxford". Ignatieff described Chatwin's sojourns there as "a prelude or epilogue to travel" and Chatwin admitted that his inability to settle, even in such a delightful place, "drives Elizabeth insane...we have everything here, but I always wish I was somewhere else. It's a condition that makes one very difficult to live with."

The art world gave Chatwin plenty of material for stories, many of which, polished from repeated tellings to his friends, he wrote down during 1988 for publication in what was to be his posthumous collection of pieces, *What Am I Doing Here*. The section of that book, 'Tales of the Art World', describes some of the people he met while working for Sotheby's, or 'Smoother-boys' as one of his friends dubbed it. The essay, 'The Duke of M-', contains a rather disagreeable anecdote about the firm's chairman, Peter Wilson, and in 'The Bey' Chatwin describes his meeting at Sotheby's with the elderly chamberlain of the exiled King of Albania who asked to be shown "something beautiful". When the young man in the grey overalls produced "a fragment of an Attic white-ground lekythos by the Achilles painter which had the most refined drawing, in golden-sepia, of a naked boy" from the collection of Lord Elgin, the Bey declared: "I see you have The Eye. I too have The Eye. We shall be friends." Chatwin describes how he managed to evade the firm's proscription on staff dealing privately (it was assumed that people like him had private incomes to supplement their low salaries, and Chatwin had to be personally warned by the Chairman). He met the Bey discreetly at his rooms at the Ritz. One object he acquired in this way was a Greek electrum ring of the fifth century. It became Elizabeth's engagement ring.

In the summer of 1962 Chatwin set out in the footsteps of his mentor Robert Byron and travelled through Afghanistan. He considered that by 1968 "the Hippies", a form of contemporary nomad he seemed to have a particular aversion to, had destroyed the country "by driving educated Afghans into the arms of the Marxists". But six years earlier on the streets of Herat you could see "men in mountainous turbans, strolling hand in hand, with roses in their mouths and rifles wrapped in flowered chintz" (*What Am I Doing Here*, p.287). Even the Afghan Embassy in London introduced you to "a world that was hilarious and strange". The visa section was run by a giant Russian émigré who had cut the lining of his jacket so that it hung, as a curtain, to hide the holes in the seat of his trousers. Chatwin tipped him with a ten-shilling note and the giant swept him off the floor in a great hug and wished him well on his trip. Chatwin gladly acknowledged that he had "slavishly" aped Byron's itinerary and, as will be seen later, his style.

In 1963 the Chairman of Sotheby's, Peter Wilson, came into Chatwin's office with Beatrice Lillie who had a picture, a Modigliani bought in New York in 1944 and stored subsequently in the attic of her house on the river at Henley-on-Thames. The firm agreed to store the picture and that Sunday Chatwin went to Beatrice Lillie's house for lunch and supper:

> We laughed, sang and Bea played the piano. I was Noel and she was Gertie. We had perfect pitch. (*What Am I Doing Here*, p.365)

In spite of such incidents, however, the excitement was not enough. As well as his disillusionment with Sotheby's he had also, since 1965 had problems with his eyesight. One day he came back from America to stay with a friend in Ireland. He drove from Dublin to Donegal and the next morning woke up blind. The sight came back in one eye during the day but when he got back to England the eye specialist warned him that he had been looking too closely at pictures and suggested that he should swap them for some long horizons. This seemed a good idea to his patient who, when asked where he wanted to go, replied, "Africa". He then claims that the specialist wrote out a prescription specifying not a new pair of spectacles but travel to Africa. The chairman, Peter Wilson, is said to have observed, " I'm sure Bruce has got something the matter with his eyes, but I can't think why he has to go to Africa." In a newspaper interview Chatwin once added a further detail: as well as the loss through temporary blindness of the one thing needful for his profession, The Eye, he also developed sores on his palms, " rather like the stigmata". The real reason for his departure was that he was "tremendously unhappy" in his job.

In July 1991 the critic David Sexton, in an attempt to call a halt to what he saw as an incipient tendency to construct a Chatwin legend, wrote in an article in the *Evening Standard* that there was " certainly a penny plain and twopence coloured version of some of the crucial events in Chatwin's life". Choosing the above incident as an example of this fictive habit among his admirers, Sexton quoted " a more humdrum account" by the diarist Kenneth Rose. The latter claimed to have been told by Chatwin that Peter Wilson had promised to make him one of three trusted young directors who would eventually run and control the firm. In the event thirteen were appointed and Chatwin walked out. It is true that others, like Howard Hodgkin, dispute this new account, and the original story may well be true. Since both Chatwin and Wilson are now dead the conflict may not prove easy to resolve.

His friends are clear about his unhappiness. Peter Levi said that " the noughts on the end of his bank account bored him" and his old schoolfriend Michael Cannon says, " he got fed up with the people. He just thought they were a lot of charlatans and two-faced." Chatwin told Colin Thubron that by the age of twenty-four he was "burnt out":

In the end I felt I might just as well be working for a rather superior

> funeral parlour. One's whole life semed to be spent valuing for probate in the apartment of somebody recently dead. There was something unbelievably sinister about all that. I imagined the things — the works of art — ricocheting down the generations, and flesh decaying all the way round them. I began to feel that works of art were literally going to kill me, there and then. (*Daily Telegraph*, 27 June 1987)

In the same interview Chatwin told Thubron that the one thing he did learn from Sotheby's was that "*things* tell you very specific stories. People own things for a series of very strange reasons. The technique of art detective work — treasure-hunting — is the way in which I research a story." But it was combing through the deaths columns of *The Times* in search of potential pickings that ultimately revolted him. "I began to feel that things, however beautiful, can also be malign," he wrote later. "The atmosphere of the art world reminded me of the morgue".

Yet, in addition to the negative recoil from the art world he was also driven by a much more positive passion for exploration. He had already travelled to some exotic places while working at Sotheby's but now embarked on what Patrick Leigh Fermor called "a frugal, ardent, and single-minded course of study". The object of his study was the nomads. In that short therapeutic period of leave after his blindness in 1966, he set off for the Sudan and trekked on camel and foot through the Red Sea hills. He found a nomad guide who made the recuperating art-expert feel "overburdened and inadequate". By the time he returned to work "a mood of fierce iconoclasm had set in" and he was determined to cut himself free permanently. He described his mood at this time to Ignatieff:

> It was at the time of the Vietnam War, and I was having to think for the first time. My career was the reverse of most people's in that I started as a rather unpleasant little capitalist in a big business in which I was extremely successful and smarmy, and suddenly I realized at the age of twenty-five or so that I was hating every minute of it. I had to change. I became quite radical and I intended to write a big radical book, which came to nothing because it was unprintable. (*Granta*, 1987)

In the jargon of his time, Chatwin was becoming "a middle

class drop-out" but first he was to have a rather unsuccessful brush with the academic world. He finally resigned from Sotheby's in 1966 (almost his last act had been to declare fake a treasury in Sofia, supposed to have been found at Troy, in the presence of "the top archaeologist of the Soviet Union") and enrolled as a first year student of archaeology at Edinburgh University. "My studies in that grim northern city were not a success," he later admitted. He did enjoy learning Sanskrit but found the archaeology "a dismal discipline — a story of technical glories interrupted by catastrophe, whereas the great figures of history were invisible." One day, while excavating a Bronze Age burial he was about to brush the earth off a skeleton when he recalled the lines on Shakespeare's tomb and knew, for a second time, that he must quit. He had got into the same trap as he had with the art-world: a dependence on *things*. He later explained: "All evidence had to be taken from inanimate objects. What interested me most were the people who had escaped the archaeological record — the nomads who trod lightly on the earth and didn't build pyramids." He had spent his summer vacations on nomadic expeditions in the central Asian steppes, which was what he loved most, not the steep banks of seats in a lecture theatre of note-taking undergraduates. Peter Levi says that he was "already past the student stage" and suggests that the snobbish democrat found that "the audience at lectures smelt". Moreover, he was displeased to be told that there are no ancient works of art, only artefacts.

Chatwin now threw himself into writing his unwriteable book called 'The Nomadic Alternative' (the title survives as a chapter he wrote for an exhibition catalogue) which was also an 'Anatomy of Restlessness'. The themes and obsessions he would chase for the remainder of his life were established in his mind but his first book was still more than a decade away. He intended the nomad book to be "wildly ambitious and intolerant" but as it grew and grew it became less and less intelligible even to its author who eventually conceded it was unpublishable. It even included "a diatribe against the act of writing itself". The essence of the book nonetheless survives in the notebook passages of *The Songlines* and Chatwin has also given us a summary of what it would have been about:

The argument, roughly, was as follows: that in becoming human, man had acquired, together with his straight legs and striding walk, a migratory 'drive' or instinct to walk long distances through the seasons; that this 'drive' was inseparable from his central nervous system; and that, when warped in conditions of settlement, it found outlets in violence, greed, status-seeking or a mania for the new. This would explain why mobile societies such as the gypsies were egalitarian, thing-free and resistant to change; also why, to reestablish the harmony of the First State, all the great teachers: — Christ, Buddha, Lao-tse, St Francis — had set the perpetual pilgrimage at the heart of their message and told their disciples, literally, to, follow The Way. (Chatwin, 1983)

This succinct statement — a sort of quintessence of Chatwinism — provides a valuable key to his writing.

As a student Chatwin must have struck his fellow undergraduates as rather different. As well as the gap in age, his experience of international travel and the art world must have made him profoundly untypical. He continued to travel before, during, and after his period as a student and we can only guess at his itinerary. In 1967 he visited the Soviet Union, looking at archaeological museums and getting terribly drunk at an Uzbeg banquet. He visited Prague and met the man who provided the model for Kaspar Joachim Utz. In August 1968 he was in Kiev and in 1969 he records another uncomfortable brush with a hippy on the campus at Berkeley, California. In 1970 he stood up at a public lecture in London where Arthur Koestler was "airing his opinion that the human species was mad" and asked why there was any difference between Koestler's view that man was contemplating his destruction as a species and the end-of-the-world predictions of the year A.D.1000. "Because one was a fantasy and the H-Bomb was real," snapped Koestler (*The Songlines*, p.237).

In the same year Chatwin was responsible for co-organising an exhibition sponsored by the Asia Society of New York, called 'The Animal Style'. In the exhibition catalogue, published in 1970, he is described as being "connected with the University of Edinburgh" but it is far more likely to have been his connections with the international art and antiquity scene that got this particular undergraduate the job. The Animal Style is the name given to the animal motif art of the nomads of the Euro-Asian steppes which flourished from China to Ireland during the Iron

Age, and, later, in the barbarian art of the Migrations Period. Chatwin's other collaborators were Dr Ann Farkas of Columbia University's Department of Art History and Archaeology and Emma Bunker of Denver Art Museum. There is very clear evidence from the catalogue of some underlying tensions between the parts of this editorial *troika*. The director of the Asia House Gallery in New York, where the exhibition opened in the winter of 1970, Gordon Bailey Washburn, writes in a foreword, with some strain, that "Mr Chatwin, an anthropologist at heart, is inclined to find shamanism the most likely inspiration for the Animal Style.... Mrs Bunker and Dr Farkas are less interested in an unprovable hypothesis and more concerned with the exacting research that traces the movements of ancient peoples and their styles of ornament...". Having delivered a tart academic rebuke to Chatwin's "unprovable hypothesis" the catalogue proceeds in a careful taxonomic spirit with occasional contributions by Chatwin (who must have winced at his colleagues' view of the nomads as "illiterate barbarians") until we reach page 175. Banished to the final chapter of the catalogue, Chatwin begins 'The Nomadic Alternative' with a sentence that instantly separates him from his collaborators and carries his unmistakeable personal signature:

> Diogenes the Cynic said that men first crowded into cities to escape the fury of those outside. Locked within their walls, they committed every outrage against one another as if this were the sole object of their coming together.

This is Chatwin's first significant piece of published writing and shows him in full command of a style that combines his customary lapidary grace with that speculative boldness that was always inseparable from it: "The City as such, appeared with astonishing abruptness out of the alluvium of Southern Mesopotamia in the late fourth millenium B.C.", is a characteristic sentence. The essay is essentially a description of nomadism and a proposal that its art is rooted in shamanism which makes it "portable, asymmetric, discordant, restless, incorporeal, and intuitive" in contrast to the "static, solid and symmetrical" art of urban civilizations. It is also written by someone who has ventured out of the library and the museum: "The steppe is brilliant with spring flowers in May. At other seasons the featureless landscape is dry and dusty or leaden with frost and snow. The nomad craves colour. He is also traditionally drawn to the reassuring brilliance of gold."

At this time Chatwin was pursuing his explorations and encounters with nomads in the field. In June 1969 he set off once more for Afghanistan with his friend Peter Levi whom he had first met while at Sotheby's. He makes an appearance, initially as "my friend Bruce", in Levi's account of his journey in search of evidence of the possible Greek occupation of Afghanistan that was published in 1972 as *The Light Garden of the Angel King*. Chatwin's photograph of Levi on a mule adorns the jacket of the Penguin Travel Library reprint of 1984. The pair flew out from London to Istanbul on 17 June 1969 for a three month trip which included revisiting some places — like the tomb of Babur at Kabul — which Chatwin had visited on earlier trips. They obviously amused each other, mixing archaeological and anthropological research with light-hearted observations on such matters as the iconography of Afghan lorries — and there is the occasional cameo of Levi's companion ("a specialist in the study of nomadic peoples"), for instance during a period where they were both briefly rather ill:

> He sat dazed on his bed dressed in a long Arab gown, reading fearsome sentences from the Royal Geographical Society's *Traveller's Guide to Health*, such as "after collapse, death soon ensues" (*The Light Garden of the Angel King*, p.72)

On another occasion Chatwin set off into the covered bazaars of Herat in pursuit of a rumour of an ancient gilt or golden crown for sale in the jewellery bazaar. He spent hours on this quest until he finally located, not the rumoured crown but a British hussar's brass helmet. Halfway through the trip they were joined by Bruce's wife, Elizabeth, who was collected at Kabul airport. Levi observed in a footnote:

> ...Bruce's wife comes from New England and is called Elizabeth. She had never been to Asia before. Anyone who thinks of bringing his wife on a journey like this should be warned that Elizabeth has unusual qualities. (*Ibid*, p.133)

One night she read both of them to sleep with some Dante.

The travel writer and novelist Colin Thubron has said that he

always travels alone, as a point of principle, but Chatwin sometimes travelled with companions like Levi or Salman Rushdie. It
is only in Patagonia and Benin where there seems to be clear
evidence in the writing that he was mostly alone. He seems to
have been naturally gregarious in spite of his fondness for
going off almost anywhere at a moment's notice. During his
'nomad period', Chatwin also visited Mauritania and in 1971 he
paid his first visit to the West African kingdom of Dahomey
and found out about the Brazilian slave millionaire Dom Francisco Felix de Souza. But he still had no fixed employment and
funds were running low. He later described himself at this point
as " penniless, depressed, and a total failure at the age of 33".

He was rescued by Francis Wyndham, a man he was later to
describe as " friend, guide and source of faultless literary judgements". Wyndham was an assistant editor of *The Sunday Times
Magazine* and offered him a job as an adviser on art and architecture but that was soon forgotten about and Chatwin took on
instead all sorts of commissions. He claimed that all his journal-
istic pieces — certainly those he chose to reprint — were " my
ideas" (with the exception of a piece on Mrs Ghandi). The best
of these pieces are to be found in the collection *What Am I Doing
Here* and their range and discursive length show them to belong
to a more expansive period in weekly journalism. Chatwin
wrote for *The Sunday Times Magazine* on a variety of subjects and
one of his earliest pieces was on the legendary Paris *couturier*,
Madeleine Vionnet whom he visited at her apartment in the
Seizième Arrondissement in Paris. Chatwin was, as his friend
Salman Rushdie put it, " much attracted (and attractive) to formidable ladies of a certain age" and his gallery of *grandes dames*
included Nadezhda Mandelstam, Diana Vreeland, and Maria
Reiche. Chatwin's style in these pieces is concise and often epigrammatic ("Like the dance it [couture] is an evanescent art,
but a great one") and his affection for his subjects (with the
exception of Mrs Ghandi) combines with his ability to share
their obsessions, to create a sense of their uniqueness.

Andre Malraux, whom Chatwin visited for *The Sunday Times*
in 1974, was, like the haughty and flinty outsider Maria Reiche,
another individual " estranged from the values of his class".
The interest of this piece is in Chatwin's evident fascination by
the heroic myth of the man of action which Malraux seemed to

embody but which some might approach with more wariness. There is a degree of hyperbole in Chatwin's account — Malraux, he thinks, is " one of the most original minds of our time" — and he links Malraux to De Gaulle as one of a pair of intellectuals and adventurers who were fascinated by the exercise of power "and by the role of the archetypal hero who saves his country". Chatwin seems to prefer their heroic nationalism to "specious internationalism" and he admires their putative ability to "see through the simple-mindedness of exaggerating the class struggle at the expense of national unity". As with the piece on Mrs Ghandi one senses that Chatwin was not at his most assured as a political analyst. Salman Rushdie once observed: " Bruce's politics could be, to put it politely, a little innocent." The piece ends with Chatwin commiserating with Malraux over the shrinking platform for heroic adventurers in the contemporary world. " There are blocks of flats in Samarkand," observes Malraux glumly.

His piece on Mrs Ghandi is distinctly unflattering. She is shown as manipulative and over-aware of her image. She " knew exactly how to time the intervals between her smiles". Yet Chatwin perceived a vulnerability beneath this outward bravado: "Politically she was a catastrophe: yet she was still the little girl who wanted to be Joan of Arc. I loved her for that — and still do." Magnus Linklater, who edited *The Sunday Times Magazine* during Chatwin's time as a contributor, recalls:

> One of his best trips for us was the one he did to India in search of an alleged wolf-child ["Shamdev: the Wolf Boy"] and to interview Indira Gandhi. He told a very funny story on his return about Indira, whom he did not consider very bright. He was telling her about the wolf child and about how it had not learned to speak until it was six years old. "Oh, that's not surprising," said Mrs Gandhi, "Sanjay did not speak properly until he was at least seven." Then, as Bruce told it, she suddenly realised what she had said and was covered in confusion.

Chatwin was deeply impressed with the Indian Foreign Minister, Atal Behri Vajpayee, who appears to have been the sort of distinctive, patrician individual he always admired: " His audience clung to every word. The level of discourse made Western electioneering seem like some barbaric rout. This was true democracy." Chatwin's account of this performance contrasts with his Coriolanus-like account of the ordinary people with their "outstretched palms and betel-stained mouths".

More satisfying, perhaps, than these political profiles are those essays where art is the subject matter. His 1973 piece on George Costakis, the leading private art collector in the Soviet Union at that time, whose collection of Leftist art from the earliest days of the Revolution was unique, is a vivid and informed account of Russian Futurism. He showed real sympathy for the Russian artists and a society where the painter had the status of "prophet and teacher", in contrast to the West where, as Chatwin of all people would know, "a revolutionary art is defused by the patronage of the rich". Although he recognised that the Futurists' "posturing" was "of the essence of middle-class revolt" he was fascinated by the streak of literal iconoclasm in the Leftist abstract art movement, linking it to his own perceptions about the nomads: "Anarchic peoples, like desert nomads, hate and destroy images, and a similar image-breaking streak runs through Russian history. The apparent endlessness of the country encourages the search for inner freedom...". Chatwin wrote that the artists and architects of the Left are recognised today as "great original geniuses" but he saw, with some sadness, that it failed in its original intent of winning a wider audience: "By their own admission they decided what the people should want, not what it did want."

He also wrote for the *The Sunday Times* a characteristic piece of speculative scholarship — a blend of history, sweeping hypothesis and fine writing — which tried to identify the actual breed of horse that the Emperor Wu-ti (145-87 B.C.) procured from the King of Ferghana, the so-called Heavenly Horses that the Emperor coveted with a monomaniac passion. And in 1973 Chatwin made a trip for the paper to Algeria and Marseilles which produced a fine and impassioned piece called 'The Very Sad Story of Salah Bougrine'. It is a disturbing portrait of French anti-Arab racism focused on a racial murder in Marseilles and revealing Chatwin's clear and felt sympathy with the underdog.

Chatwin worked for *The Sunday Times Magazine* as a freelance contributor, paid a retainer of what in those days would have been a handsome £2,000 a year. He is said to have announced his departure with a sudden telegram to his employers announcing: GONE TO PATAGONIA FOR SIX MONTHS. The editor of the magazine, Magnus Linklater, now editor of *The Scotsman*, knows nothing of this story. Nor does his successor, Hunter Davies, who took over in 1975. "If he did send it," says Linklater, "it was not on leaving the magazine because he was only ever a freelance contributor." Francis Wyndham, who might have been a recipient of the telegram, says: " It must be a fiction". He says that Chatwin never mentioned it to him and he only heard of the story later "as a sort of *Sunday Times* myth". Linklater confirms that Chatwin was a very valued contributor: " Bruce was certainly one of the jewels in our crown."

Hunter Davies, however, was less enthusiastic and it is clear that if the telegram announcing Chatwin's departure did not exist it might well have been necessary to invent it. For Hunter Davies, the magazine's new editor, had been given a brief that did not include a future for Chatwin. Davies says he inherited Chatwin as one of a handful of contract writers, most of whom he dumped, including Jeff Bernard ("who had written bugger all for at least two years"). Chatwin might have resigned first, he recalls, but he would not have kept him anyway because he had a new brief from the paper's overall editor, Harold Evans, to change the format "going more for home-based, shorter stories, bringing in a new section called Lifespan". Davies adds bluntly: "I did not care for his purple prose which I thought poncy and self-indulgent for our purposes... I vaguely remember talking to him in the office, telling him the new format, and he seemed very off hand and superior, then he went orf. To Patagonia?"

Chatwin was thirty-five and a writer of proven ability but he had still not produced a book. His trip to Patagonia was to result two years later in one of the most strikingly original post-war English travel books and to launch him on a writing career that, owing to his tragic illness, was to last barely more than a decade.

3. WILD DENIZENS

Why Patagonia? In choosing what he called this "country of black fogs and whirlwinds at the end of the habited world" as the subject of his first book, Chatwin was motivated partly by a childhood longing, partly by an accidental meeting in Paris with a nonagenarian architect and designer, and partly by the glimpse of a commission from the *Sunday Times*.

His editor at *The Sunday Times Magazine*, Magnus Linklater, recalls that Chatwin suggested a piece for the magazine which would trace the trail of the real Butch Cassidy and the Sundance Kid who in 1900 decided to follow a rumour that the southern tip of the American continent offered the kind of outlaw freedom characteristic of 1870s Wyoming. This would involve him going from north to south America and Linklater is almost certain he commissioned Chatwin to write it. Somewhere along the trail other obsessions took over and, as his former editor puts it: "A *Sunday Times Magazine* assignment, therefore, disappeared and was later transmuted into *In Patagonia*... I remember thinking it was entirely typical that he should stray so far from the original plan. A Bruce Chatwin assignment was always unpredictable."

At about the same time, just before he left the paper, Chatwin was in Paris visiting the ninety-three-year-old architect and designer Eileen Gray in whose salon in the Rue de Bonaparte hung a map of Patagonia which she had painted in gouache (and which Chatwin was later to inherit). He told her that he had always wanted to go there. "So have I," she added. "Go there for me." This was the decisive moment, he says, when the GONE TO PATAGONIA telegram was despatched from Paris.

But the most powerful motivation was the story with which the book opened. His grandmother kept in her glass-fronted cabinet of curiosities a piece of animal skin with coarse reddish hair, stuck to a card with a rusty pin. Bruce was told, mistakenly he was later to discover, that it was a piece of brontosaurus skin procured by her cousin Charley Milward the sailor, one of the footloose Chatwin ancestors, "an eccentric, somewhat peppery" captain of the New Zealand Shipping Company. Charley's first command was wrecked at Desolation Island, at the entrance to the Strait of Magellan, in 1898. While salvaging the wreck he was seduced by this remote country and settled in the port of Punta Arenas, buying a share in an iron foundry. In 1904 he became British consul in which capacity he once played host to the explorer Sir Ernest Shackleton. Charley found his 'brontosaurus' perfectly preserved in a glacier in Tierra del Fuego and had it salted, packed in barrels and sent to the Natural History Museum in South Kensington. On the voyage through the tropics, however, it decomposed and what eventually reached the museum was a heap of bones. A fragment of the skin, however, was sent to Chatwin's grandmother by post. The whole story, it turns out, was a farrago. What was in the cabinet was a piece of mylodon or giant sloth whose skin and bones were found conserved in a cave at Last Hope Sound in the Chilean province of Magallanes. Also preserved by the dryness and salt were pieces of the beast's excrement, some of which Chatwin brought home and kept — until his charlady accidentally threw them out.

All this might have been sufficient provocation to a conventional travel writer but Chatwin could never be summed up adequately by that label and had other spurs to his imagination. In an entertainment he and the writer Paul Theroux were later to stage at the Royal Geographical Society and which was subsequently published as *Patagonia Revisited* (1985) he declared: " if we are travellers at all, we are literary travellers. A literary reference or connection is likely to excite us as much as a rare animal or plant...". In spite of the vivid, pictorial quality of Chatwin's writing, and in spite of his ability to see the world clearly and sharply, all his stories are filtered through a rich screen of literary allusion and reference. He travelled light but there was always room in his leather rucksack for a book and when he set off in 1975 for his six month trip to Patagonia the Russian poet Osip Mandelstam's *Journey to Armenia* and Hemingway's collection of stories *In Our Time*, were basic rations.

Accounts of voyages to the Antarctic had influenced many English poets and Chatwin believed that Shakespeare's creation of Caliban in *The Tempest* is traceable to his reading of the account of Magellan's 1519-22 voyage by Antonio Pigafetta. Wordsworth and Coleridge read Captain Shelvocke's eighteenth century account of the shooting of an albatross off the coast of Tierra del Fuego which almost certainly influenced the writing of *The Rime of the Ancient Mariner*. More recently, a turn of the century voyage in search of the mylodon, which was thought to be still alive, "seems to have been an ingredient", in Chatwin's words, in Conan Doyle's *The Lost World*. Edgar Allan Poe's haunting *The Narrative of Arthur Gordon Pym* followed his reading of Captain James Weddell's *Voyage Towards the South Pole*. And in addition to these indirect literary influences and refractions, there were books like W.H. Hudson's *Idle Days in Patagonia* or Darwin's *Voyage of the Beagle* which provided more direct accounts. Hudson's apostrophe on landing in Patagonia is typical of how this remote place was seen:

> At last, Patagonia! How often had I pictured in imagination, wishing with an intense longing to visit this solitary wilderness, resting far off in its primitive and desolate peace, untouched by man, remote from civilisation. (Hudson, p.4)

Hudson speculated (in terms that, stripped of his period racism — he wrote blithely of "the superior race" — must surely have found an echo in Chatwin's thoughts on the cooked and the raw in civilisation) on the effect of the Patagonian solitude: "the civilised life is one of continual repression... I had undoubtedly *gone back*; and that state of intense watchfulness, or alertness rather, with suspension of the higher intellectual faculties, represented the mental state of the pure savage...my belief is that we might learn something by looking more beneath the hardened crust of custom into the still burning core..." (Hudson, pp.205, 212). Passages like these show how Patagonia functioned symbolically in the Western imagination as, in Chatwin's words "a metaphor for The Ultimate, the point beyond which one could not go". Hesketh Prichard, author of *Through the Heart of Patagonia* (1902), an account of an expedition, sponsored by the *Daily Express*, to establish the truth or otherwise of the existence of the living mylodon, summed up how Patagonia was seen at the start of the century:

> Patagonia is a country about which little is known to the world in general, books dealing with it being few and far between, while the aspect of that quaint tail of South America and its wild denizens has practically never been pictorially brought under the eye of the public.

This was the strange, resonant, almost forgotten territory that Chatwin came to in the latter part of 1975 and 1976 to write a book that was to prove, like all his subsequent books, an instant critical success, hailed by the *Times Literary Supplement* on its appearance as "a minor classic". It also represented a break from one tradition of British travel-writing (a tradition, however, that is not giving up without a struggle, as the success of a book like William Dalrymple's *In Xanadu* (1989) demonstrated). In Chatwin's book there are no funny foreigners, no Englishman-abroad slapstick, no comic restaurant menu translations, no clotted purple passages, no turgid potted history, no self-admiring derring-do, no virtuoso lists. Instead there is a condensed and episodic structure, built around a series of stories of extraordinary characters. They are not mocked or guyed but presented as individuals. Their idiosyncrasy is acutely observed and recorded. The style is racy and elliptical, the chapters of a sometimes surprising brevity. It is also a narrative from which the author himself is largely absent. Chatwin rarely wrote directly about the actual mechanics or hardships of travel. He was more interested in what he saw than the circumstances of the man who saw it.

In 1976 he bounded up the steps of the publishers Jonathan Cape in Bedford Square with the manuscript of *In Patagonia* in his rucksack. Susannah Clapp, now a member of the editorial board of the *London Review of Books* but at that time an editor at Cape, wrote, in her *Guardian* obituary, of Chatwin's arrival that morning:

> He was wearing a brilliant emerald jacket, and carrying a haversack: in it were a pocket edition of the letters of Sydney Smith, a

novel by Blaise Cendrars and the manuscript of his first book, *In Patagonia*. The books in his haversack changed from day to day; so did the pages of *In Patagonia*. Pacing the room, reading aloud to test for sound as well as sense, Chatwin would pounce on a phrase and produce a new anecdote. He would cut an entire chapter without a minute's brooding. The book that resulted redefined travel writing.

This vivid reminiscence — Clapp is soon to publish a memoir of Chatwin — conveys something of the arresting quality of Chatwin's writing as well as his personal presence. The book arrived on the scene when British travel writing was about to undergo one of its periodic revivals. But Chatwin, although a beneficiary of that publishing boom, was not the sort of travel writer who would plan a book over a publisher's lunch to meet a perceived coming demand. He would have written the books he chose to write regardless of what was going on around him. Nevertheless, he was briefly mentioned by Paul Fussell in his timely critical study of 1980, *Abroad: British Literary Travelling Between the Wars*. Fussell's book (which had the incidental benefit of rescuing the reputation of Chatwin's favourite modern travel narrative, Robert Byron's *The Road to Oxiana*) was a lament for what he saw as the golden age of literary travel before travellers became tourists and all that remained was "jet tourism among the ruins". But in spite of this critical jeremiad Chatwin showed that an inventive writer could breathe new life into an old genre. *In Patagonia* is his proof.

In trying to define just what, in literary critical terms, a travel book was, Fussell noted its frequent kinship with the quest romance (see his chapter 'Travel Books as Literary Phenomena'). That would have appealed to Chatwin as a description of his books (he used the term 'searches' to describe them) and although he admitted that it was in some sense a "spurious quest", his pursuit of the fabulous Patagonian beast of his childhood did give him the idea for the form of a travel book: "for the oldest kind of traveller's tale is one in which the narrator leaves home and goes to a far country in search of a legendary beast" (*Patagonia Revisited*, p.17)

In Patagonia had another dimension, too. "We are...fascinated by exiles," he and Theroux wrote in *Patagonia Revisited*. Patagonia, famous for its expatriate Welsh community, was host to many other voluntary and involuntary exiles who had drifted to this terminus of the civilised world. Chatwin was drawn to people at the margins, living solitary or eccentric lives, in remote places. In an interview with Melvyn Bragg on London Weekend Television's *South Bank Show* in November 1982 he observed: "I'm a great believer in the determining character of landscape on people...there you have a very bare landscape in which these figures...their eccentricities, stood out in sharp silhouette against this particular bare horizon." He protested that he "wasn't particularly looking for eccentricities", that he simply observed people as they were. Chatwin himself, in the same interview, made explicit a connection that seems obvious. Looking out of the window of a train rattling from Newport towards the Black Mountains he explained to his interviewer: "I don't see any real difference between this and Patagonia at all." The characters of *On The Black Hill* also "stood out...against this particular bare horizon" and had something of that solitary, removed quality he observed in the Patagonians. Similarly, the Jones family in *On The Black Hill*, although not strictly exiles — they lived in the land of their birth — were exiles from the major events of their time and its dominant values. The Welsh border country in Chatwin's imagination is a place apart, relatively untouched by time, where "eccentricity" — or the freedom of human beings to be what they choose to be — had, in some sense difficult to define, greater scope. Neither entirely English nor entirely Welsh it avoided the fierce identifications of nationalism and had grown used to being left to its own devices.

This theme of exile, of people living at the margins, denied the consolation of an abiding city, is treated in a literal and metaphorical sense throughout Chatwin's writing. The Brazilian slave trader, Dom Francisco da Silva, exiled in the kingdom of Dahomey in *The Viceroy of Ouidah* and with an ambiguous longing to return to Brazil; Kaspar Joachim Utz, trapped in a society whose values are not his own but which he cannot bring himself to leave; Benjamin and Lewis Jones in their Radnorshire hill farm which is a bulwark against the intrusions of the twentieth century and its historical responsibilities, are either physically or metaphorically unhoused and at a tangent to their societies — the permanent condition of the exile.

In Patagonia is written in ninety-seven short numbered sections ranging from little more than a paragraph to no more than
half a dozen pages. This is the most distinctive stylistic quality
of the book, together with its short, pared down sentences. It
was a style fully formed in this first book and one which saw no
need to develop significantly in those that followed, although it
was put to ever richer and more varied uses. If there was immature apprenticework or painful experimentation in Chatwin's
progress towards being a writer the reader has been spared it.
The evident accomplishment of this book by a writer known, if
at all, only as a writer of stylish pieces in the Sunday colour
supplements, took the reviewers by surprise. " Bruce Chatwin is
an original," wrote Maurice Richardson in the *New Statesman*.
" Laconical and elliptical and alive" was the judgement of *The
Observer* on this " brilliant" book which won both the Haw-
thornden Prize and the E.M. Forster Award of the American
Academy of Arts and Letters.

It begins with the story of the piece of pseudo-brontosaurus
skin in his grandmother's cabinet which conveys Chatwin's
childhood enthusiasm and *Boy's Own Paper* taste for old-fashioned heroes: Charley Milward the Sailor was, in Bruce's
youthful imagination "a god among men — tall, silent and
strong, with black mutton-chop whiskers and fierce blue eyes".
The picture of his grandmother is characteristic in its rapid verbal brushstrokes:

> My grandmother lived in a red-brick house set behind a screen of
> yellow-spattered laurels. It had tall chimneys, pointed gables and
> a garden of blood-coloured roses. Inside it smelled of church. (*In
> Patagonia*, p.6)

In the room there were paintings of Dutch burghers " their fat
buttery faces nesting in white ruffs", another entirely characteristic example of Chatwin's pithy phrase-making. He excelled
at description and in the placing of the incidental detail that
reveals a shaft of meaning. But he was less interested in exploring the inner life or psychologising. His characters reveal themselves through how they look and what they do or say. It is the
same with the frequent excursions into autobiography in his
books: there are some memorable anecdotes but we do not really get to know their protagonist. He would always prefer dia-

logue to interior monologue. In this opening chapter we see young Bruce's awakening passion for geography, stirred by the Cold War fears instilled by his teachers at school. "The war was coming and there was nothing we could do," the schoolboys came to feel, and Chatwin never lost that sense of potential nuclear catastrophe. The boys formed an emigration committee which pored over atlases and eventually fixed on Patagonia as the place to be after a nuclear attack. Bruce pictured the house where he would live when the rest of the world blew up. It had blazing log fires inside and, an essential detail, had "the walls lined with the best books".

This autobiographical scene-setting introduces in a couple of pages all the book's key themes: travel, escape, the fictionalising of experience, the influence of family, scientific curiosity, art, contemporary history, the determining role of the imagination and Chatwin's precocious confidence in his own judgement. The author then begins to efface himself. We cut immediately to Buenos Aires whose history, he says, is written in its telephone directory. The non-Argentine surnames tell "a story of exile, disillusion and anxiety behind lace curtains" and the city reminds him of Russia:

> the cars of the secret police bristling with aerials; women with splayed haunches licking ice-cream in dusty parks; the same bullying statues, the pie-crust architecture, the same avenues that were not quite straight, giving the illusion of endless space and leading out into nowhere. (*In Patagonia*, p.8)

The simplicity and swing of this writing is deceptive: such a style is worked at.

Chatwin also introduces, very early in his first book, another characteristic device of his writing: what we might call the technique of the corroborative anecdote which was developed to its furthest extent in *The Songlines*, a book consciously modelling itself on the eighteenth century philosophical novel in dialogue form. The pattern is that Chatwin will make an observation (in this case that Buenos Aires is reminiscent of Tsarist Russia) and conjure up, let us say, a 'friend' who is the recipient of the *aperçu* and who caps it with a corroborative observation that confirms the force of the original perception. In this case, the friend recalls the recent visit of a Russian White émigreé who excitedly explored the friend's country house, culminating in a declaration on seeing the attics: "Ah! I knew it! The smell of my childhood!" In *The Songlines* this technique can sometimes come to seem a little self-serving as Chatwin is seen repeatedly getting there first and having his understanding of a particular point triumphantly endorsed by some appreciative listener. The effect can be to render him too clever by half or to show up someone else as being a little slower off the mark or caught out in some imperfect grasp (of Aboriginal lore or myth perhaps) which exiles him from the court of the initiated to which Chatwin is seen to belong by right. It can be defended, perhaps, by its paternity in the form of the dialogue novel chosen by Chatwin as a means of conveying complex material in a light, easily digestible form whose alternative might be pages of interminable exposition. Brevity and lightness of touch was always his goal.

From Buenos Aires Chatwin took the train to La Plata. There is little detail in the book about such journeys, how they were made, or what happened along the way or what discomfort they might have caused the traveller — details which in the conventional travel book would loom large. But the one detail from that railway journey he does mention is strikingly efficient. In the compartment are two "everyday victims of *machismo*", a thin woman with a black eye and a sickly teenage girl clinging to her dress.

> Sitting opposite was a boy with green squiggles on his shirt. I looked again and saw the squiggles were knife blades. (*In Patagonia*, p.9)

In La Plata Chatwin brings on the first of his cast of Patagonian 'characters'. Florentino Ameghino, who was Director of the National Museum at his death, was "a solitary autodidact" who with a Chatwinian boldness "took on the entire body of scientific opinion" by trying to prove that all hot-blooded mammals began in South America and went north (natural historians believed the traffic to have gone in the opposite direction). After a good dose of natural history and Linnaean Latin in the La Plata museum, Chatwin headed back to Buenos Aires to catch the night bus south. His exploration of the Patagonian back country had begun. He meets a man called Bill Philips who drives him to his remote cottage to talk about Turgenev and then takes him to Bahia Blanca, the last big place before the Patagonian Desert. Already the tension between the native Indians and the gringos is apparent, the former living in shacks and the latter enjoying what prosperity the land yields. The desert, writes Chatwin, has not produced "any dramatic excesses of the spirit" and seems peculiarly bleak with "land and sky dissolving into an absence of colour". Darwin was haunted by its arid wastes and W.H. Hudson concluded here "that desert wanderers discover in themselves a primeval calmness".

The first of the interspersed stories is that of H.R.H. Prince Philippe of Araucania and Patagonia who granted Chatwin an audience one drizzling November at his public relations firm in Paris. The exiled king was engaged in trying to publish manuscripts justifying his claims and Chatwin presents an encapsulated history of the aspirant kings. The prince, however, was later to describe *In Patagonia* as "an unfortunate book".

Continuing on his way south, Chatwin encounters the expatriate Welsh:

> They were poor people in search of a New Wales, refugees from a failed independence movement, and from Parliament's ban on Welsh in schools.... They chose Patagonia for its absolute remoteness and foul climate; they did not want to get rich. (*In Patagonia*, p.24)

In observing the Patagonian Welsh, Chatwin's eye for the incongruous yields pictures of a Welsh boarding house owned by Italians who play Neapolitan songs on a juke-box; Mrs Jones of Bangor who, in her teashop, discovers with the writer a mutual acquaintance from her home town and declares: "It's a small world"; Mr and Mrs Powell whom Chatwin has to help to identify Caernarfon on their tea-towel map of Wales; the Davies family in their living room unchanged since 1913 (prefiguring The Vision farmhouse in *On The Black Hill*); and the brick chapel where Welsh hymns are sung: "The Welshmen cheered up all who saw their bright and weatherbeaten faces." He also meets strange, sad, artistic geniuses: Anselmo the pianist ("you could imagine you were in the presence of a genius") and the unnamed poet whose epic verses enchant the writer ("the scope of

his verses was cosmic"). As well as the Welsh there are characters like Jim Ponsonby, the "perfect English gentleman" with
his Hereford bulls; or the Iranian at the Bahai Institute of
Trevelin whose questioning of Chatwin about his religion
prompted the reply: "My God is the God of Walkers. If you
walk hard enough, you probably don't need any other God."
An exiled German raises a toast to Ludwig the Mad and a Scot
tries to preserve at his sheep-station "the dried-up skeleton of a
thistle".

And so the catalogue of stranded, unique, characters runs on.
Always Chatwin finds marvellously compressed phrases to
flick them into life: the Lithuanian he finds at lunch " ladling
the bortsch into the ivory orb of his skull" or the moody
younger son of an *estancia*: " the accordion of his forehead
whined a story of immobility and repressed ambition". Sometimes the book starts to look like the front office of a theatrical
agent spending an afternoon auditioning character actors. They
come thick and fast so that the 'eccentric' can, after a time, come
to seem the norm.

The book also breaks off from time to time to explore at
greater length the adventures of Butch Cassidy, for example
(who wrote in a letter: "I am a long way from civilisation"). Or
to tell the story of the Elizabethan voyagers; the 1920-21 Anarchist revolution led by Antonio Soto; the masonic sect of male
witches in Chiloe; Darwin's voyage; and, of course, the story of
Charley Milward himself, which draws on some of Charley's
own written stories. The climax of *In Patagonia* is Chatwin's
arrival at the mylodon cave at Last Hope Sound where the piece
of skin in his grandmother's cabinet originated. But it is an anti-
climax. "I had accomplished the object of this ridiculous journey," declares the author as he stoops to pick up a piece of the
familiar coarse reddish hair. The object of the quest suddenly
seems irrelevant compared with what has been seen and heard
along the way. The book ends with his taking ship from Punta
Arenas with a satisfying complement of madmen.

In *On The Black Hill*, the painter Nigel Lambert is fond of telling tall stories about his involvement in the Spanish War, confident of an audience that " knew nothing of Spain and couldn't
check the details of his stories". But there were some who accused Chatwin of precisely that. In 1991 John Pilkington pub-

lished *An Englishman in Patagonia*, a rather pedestrian travel book which seemed determined not to allow itself to be put in the shade by the literary quality of its predecessor ("Like Flaubert, Chatwin never tired of exploring the Aladdin's Cave of theatrical possibility which life opened up" is a characteristic sentence). It sought to cast the brisk, unillusioned eye of the backpacker over some of Chatwin's observations. Pilkington marshalled a certain amount of evidence, not all of it conclusive, that put a question mark over the veracity of some of the things the writer described. Chatwin, he demonstrated, was fibbing when he described the entrance of Eberhardt's cave as four hundred feet wide. Pilkington's careful pacing found it to be "no more than 100". More seriously, perhaps, he quoted from *The Bulletin*, a monthly journal published by the British Community Council of Argentina which revealed a deep hostility towards Chatwin as a result of *In Patagonia* in the course of a review of *The Songlines*. It seems that at least some Patagonians were not very keen on the picture *In Patagonia* had painted and when Pilkington's book was published Chatwin's alleged unreliability as a witness attracted some attention in national newspapers. Susannah Clapp, one of Chatwin's literary executors, dismissed these charges and was quoted in the *Daily Telegraph* as saying: "I don't think anyone supposed *In Patagonia* was a straight travelogue — it's too interesting for that." With his first book, the question of the relation of truth to fiction had been raised and would remain a constant preoccupation of critics.

But in 1977 Chatwin could bask in the success of his first book which the *Daily Telegraph* reviewer, David Holloway, called "the most original travel book to be published for some time". What none of the reviewers could have predicted was that Chatwin's potential for surprise had not been exhausted. Original as *In Patagonia* was, his next book was equally distinctive and turned its back on the option of more of the same or milking a successfully proven formula.

* * *

In 1978, with the success of his first book, *In Patagonia*, assured, Bruce Chatwin made his second visit to the West African kingdom of Dahomey, now transformed by Mathieu Kerekov's 1972 Marxist coup into The People's Republic of Benin. Like Patagonia, Dahomey already had a place in the literary imagination where it functioned as an image of extreme barbarism. Tennyson wrote in a very late poem, 'The Dawn', of: "Head-hunters and boats of Dahomey that float upon human blood", his source being the traveller Sir Richard Burton's *A Mission to Gelele, King of Dahome* (1864), a copy of which the poet owned and which it is likely that Chatwin read (although there is no evidence that he knew Tennyson's poem). In that book Burton discusses, admittedly with some scepticism, a report "that the king floated a canoe and paddled himself in a tank full of human blood" (*The Poems of Tennyson*, ed. Christopher Ricks, p 1453, n.).

Chatwin described the Kingdom of Dahomey in the last century as "a Black Sparta squeezed between the Yoruba tribes of present-day Nigeria and the Ewe tribes of Togo". When he made his first visit in January 1971 it was still called Dahomey and the capital Cotonou was still "a town of belly laughs and French brassieres". That phrase comes from the preface to the first edition of *The Viceroy of Ouidah* which explained the background to the book's composition but which was silently omitted from subsequent paperback editions, presumably to encourage a focus on its fictionality. Chatwin visited the decaying slave towns of the coast — Ouidah, Porto Novo, Grand Popo — which were known collectively as Little Brazil. He learned of the Brazilian slave trader, Dom Francisco Felix de Souza, whose grand house was now ruinous. The latter died a madman and was buried under his Goanese four-poster bed in a barrel of rum. In a piece written in 1988 for the magazine *Interview* Chatwin observed coolly: "Here plainly was a story worth telling".

It was also a story tailor-made for Chatwin's peculiar talents. The mild eccentricities of the Patagonians were as nothing compared to the rococo barbarisms of the Dahomean kings and with the life of de Souza the writer's imagination could let itself rip. Originally, however, he intended the book to be a work of nonfiction and his second trip in 1978 was made with the intention of collecting material for a life of the slaver:

> All went well with my research until, one Sunday morning, my taxi happened to be travelling in the opposite direction to a plane-load of mercenaries who had landed at Cotonou airport and were shooting their way towards the Presidential Palace. The driver exclaimed, 'C'est la guerre!' and turned the car round, only to fall in

with a unit of the Benin Army. I was arrested as a mercenary: the real mercenaries retreated back to the airport and flew off (*The Viceroy of Ouidah*, p.2, first edition).

The next two days, Chatwin continued, "I would prefer to forget". He later wrote a fictionalised account, 'A Coup', of his capture by the military. This piece, originally written for *Granta*, appears in *What Am I Doing Here* as one of a number of pieces each subtitled 'a story'. That term, in the writer's words, "is intended to alert the reader to the fact that, however closely the narrative may fit the facts, the fictional process has been at work". Whenever it is possible to check (by, for example, placing a 'factual' autobiographical piece of writing alongside its fictionalised counterpart) Chatwin seems to have kept pretty close to the 'facts' (although these themselves may have been the occasion of his most ardent fictionalising). Once again, the distinction between fiction and non-fiction in Chatwin's writing had come to the fore. Where his previous book had attracted some local censure in Argentina for its alleged distortions, the issue was now becoming a matter of the protocols of literary genre. At any rate, the story of the coup begins, like the account in the preface, at seven on a Sunday morning. It fills in what happened after Chatwin's arrest. What looked like a firing squad was assembling outside the guardroom and, after a threatening insurgent colonel is rapidly replaced by an equally intimidating Amazon colonel, the writer is instructed to remove his trousers (revealing a pair of pink and white boxer shorts from Brooks Brothers) and is put up against a wall while a crowd chants: "*Mort aux mercenaires!*" He passes out in the heat and is eventually driven to another barracks where after a horrifying night he is released at last. The French water engineer Jacques captured with him observes laconically: "You have material."

A week after this experience Chatwin was in Rio de Janeiro following up the Brazilian aspects of his story and he never returned to Benin. The country had left him nonetheless with "the bones of the story and a number of vivid impressions". As a boy he had read accounts of King Gezo's Amazons and various accounts by Victorian travellers of human sacrifice. He had also met Pierre Verger "the master of Afro-Brazilian studies" and read his seminal book on the slave trade between Benin and Bahia. He had also met descendants of the de Souzas. But in the end he concluded that such was the patchiness of his material his best strategy was to change the names of the principal characters and to go on to write "a work of the imagination". He could not quite bring himself to call it a novel.

"Since it was impossible to fathom the alien mentality of my characters," he wrote, "my only hope was to advance the narrative in a sequence of cinematographic images and here I was strongly influenced by the films of Werner Herzog." He remembered saying that if *The Viceroy of Ouidah* were ever made into a movie "only Herzog could do it" which is exactly what he eventually did. The film, *Cobra Verde*, was a riot of Herzogian excess (Chatwin has described the memorable anarchy of life on the set) and was to be judged by at least one critic, in the *Spectator*, as "preposterous". Chatwin claimed that his book appeared in 1980 "to the bemusement of reviewers, some of whom found its cruelties and baroque prose unstomachable". In fact, the reviews were glowing. Graham Hough in *The London Review of Books* called it "a grimly remarkable piece of writing" and Jan Morris in *The Times'* annual 'Critic's Choice' "a bizarre tour de force". The chorus was once again unanimous in its praise. Reviewers noted the book's brevity, its stylistic brilliance, and the vividness of its imagery. As Andrew Sinclair put it in *The Times*: "He can create an exotic atmosphere with a few disconnected sentences that glitter like a Byzantine mosaic and make sense by their very apartness." With references back to his brilliant debut, reviewers now started to place Chatwin. Graham Greene, Joseph Conrad and Malcolm Lowry were mentioned as precursors in a tradition of English imagining of exotic excess. Auberon Waugh thought it was as "funny" as his father's *Black Mischief* but the book is surely darker and closer to the spirit of Conrad's *Heart of Darkness*. Chatwin's book, however, lacks the brooding metaphysical depth of Conrad's novel and avoids, scrupulously, any authorial interventions or oblique commentaries that would attempt to draw out its significances. The fastidious 'cinematic' rendering is not objective — Chatwin's descriptions are highly coloured and idiosyncratic — but the resulting picture is intended to speak for itself. There is no particular moral revulsion at the slave trade, only vivid portrayal of the decadent splendour of Dahomey and the life-style of the slavers. The "unstomachable" aspect of the book lies perhaps in its brilliantly amoral technique, its aesthetic relish in rendering barbarism beautiful. Chatwin's style was described by one of his obituarists as "jewelled" and "heartless" — a rather mannered formulation, perhaps, but one which exposes the writer to the charge of lack of feeling. That the style *was* brilliant was not in question. Chatwin had established himself as a writer who knew how to make a striking effect.

The now familiar gift for phrase making is immediately on display in the opening pages where the descendants of de Souza/da Silva are gathered to celebrate Dom Francisco's memory at a requiem Mass. There is Father Olimpio da Silva, for example, "swivelling his luminous bronze head with the authority of a gun-turret" and the little girls whose hair is "balkanised into zones". Side by side with the usual spareness and economy there is that other dimension of Chatwin's style: the love of particularity and precise description of things which sends the reader scurrying to the dictionary to puzzle out such words as "harmattan" and "caladium". The description of the "unctuous" feast which follows the Mass affords the opportunity for more luscious vocabulary. Discussing the book in *The London Review of Books*, Karl Miller (one of Chatwin's most stringent critics) said that this passage was "like the jewelled prose of the upper-class English traveller, carried to the threshold of burlesque — and maybe across it, to produce a variety of Camp".

The first of the six sections or movements which make up the book thus establishes the scene: the sense of decline in this extraordinary clan, the weight of its history, and the bizarre but static splendour of its rituals and processions which contrast with the absurd present day Marxist-Leninist rhetoric crackling out of the public radios.

After the dramatic opening picture and the glimpse of Dom Francisco's dying daughter Eugenia ("a skeleton who happened to breathe") the action begins to travel backwards. In his previous book Chatwin had made episodic attempts at recreating the past but here his historical imagination is given full rein. His technique of reanimating the past by making it seem contemporary is achieved through vivid word-painting that has about it a sharp sense of actuality, as if he were projecting on to the historical screen the observations of today. The youthful Eugenia is brought alive like this: "The corners of her mouth lifted in a perpetual smile from pronouncing the slurred, suggestive consonants of Brazilian Portugese". The specificity is such that Chatwin must have had some original in mind from his researches in Brazil. After being seduced and abandoned by an English officer Eugenia retreats into a world of her own and the da Silvas fortunes sink with the decline of the slave trade. In a fugitive premonition of *On The Black Hill* she cherishes a Church Missionary Society print beckoning the traveller up The Straight and Narrow Path together with a panorama of Bahia "which reminded her of the New Jerusalem". *In Patagonia* introduced Chatwin's great theme of human restlessness, and his second book focuses on the life of another restless spirit.

The third section of the book goes right back to the beginning with the birth of Dom Francisco in the dry, scrubby cattle country of the Brazilian north east. Like Lewis Jones's grounded dream of flight, his family, "like all people born in thorny places...dream of green fields and a life of ease". His mother takes up with a half-breed who is by instinct a wanderer. As she watches his restlessness "her fingers would claw the table top and the splinters got under her nails" — an example of what V.S. Pritchett called Chatwin's "power to bring human feeling to the sight by some casual action". Dom Francisco becomes a wanderer in turn after his mother's death and the subsequent death of the half-breed. Moreover, there is a callousness about him: "His own sufferings had hardened him to the sufferings of others". He spends seven years (roughly the amount of time Chatwin spent from abandoning his studies to the publication of his first book) drifting through the backlands of the Brazilian north east doing odd jobs:

Sometimes he knew a flash of happiness, but only if it was time to be departing. (*Viceroy of Ouidah*, p.53)

He meets the itinerant Robin Hood-like bandit known as Cobra Verde who walks eighteen leagues a day, "and he too believed he would go on wandering for ever". He nonetheless marries and tries to settle down on a ranch but soon begins to give signs of a suppressed violence. He also shows an odd and exaggerated fear of the moment of birth which hints at his alienation from ordinary human relationships and preoccupations, as well as from a domicile. He is soon back on the road "believing any set of four walls to be a tomb or trap". He becomes a permanent outsider who passes other people's houses, craving "their simple pleasures of touch and trust", but always repulsed. He is not just a stranger to settled society but to conventional sexuality and when he eventually drifts to Bahia his sensual experiments are bisexual and unhappy: "They left him with the sensation of having brushed with death: none came back a second time". The compression and pace of this narrative of Dom Francisco's early life are remarkable and have something of the quality of an epic narrative.

The fourth section of the book tells of the arrival at Ouidah which was "passing through one of its periodic bouts of turmoil". Dom Francisco takes to the slave trade and to the paradox of settlement: "Having always thought of himself as a footloose wanderer, he now became a patriot and man of property". As he grows rich he persists in the belief that his native country, Brazil, will reward him and dreams of Bahia in spite of "a presentiment that he would never get out of Africa". The condition of exile slowly engulfs him:

> Gradually, Africa swamped him and drew him under. Perhaps out of loneliness, perhaps in despair of fighting the climate, he stepped into the habits of the natives. (*Viceroy of Ouidah*, p.79)

He also becomes involved with the King and eventually, after copious descriptions of the monarch's ghoulish buffooneries, and after Dom Francisco's imprisonment, the two men swear a blood pact which has the resonance of a Faustian compact:

> Francisco Manuel drank with the lightheartedness of the man who has skipped from certain death. It took another thirty years for him to realize the extent of his obligatons. (*Viceroy of Ouidah*, p.90)

The penultimate section shows Dom Francisco contemplating a doomed attempt to escape his situation: "He wanted to get out, to forget, to begin again." But the wish for revenge against the King for destroying his trade is stronger and he begins to solicit the monarch, who makes him his Viceroy at Ouidah. Although he assumed the manners and style of a Brazilian seigneur: " Each year, with the dry season, he would slough off the habits of civilisation and go to war." He enters a "self-directed nightmare" of heartless violence and cruelty that is the mirror image of the King's lust to acquire more skulls. In peacetime, the desire to construct a Brazilian *casa grande* is of a piece with his reading of the Brazilian newspapers and his search for honours at home which are denied him because his trade has become something from which the Brazilians now wish to be distanced. He plans to return but his citizenship has lapsed and when permission eventually comes he is bankrupt. Eventually he goes mad, scribbles "incoherent prophecies" and talks to the waves on the beach, destroyed by the growth of Abolitionism and competition from " the Brazilians" (returned black ex-slaves).

The brief final section shows his daughter remembering, as she lies dying, the death of Dom Francisco and his burial in a barrel of rum with the heads of two sacrificed children. The ornate and cruel story has come to an end. The unsparing detail, the absence of judgement, the steady rhythms of Chatwin's prose give the story a sense of tragic inevitability, of the downfall of a rootless man, a trapped wanderer. Nothing, however, in this brilliantly macabre tale could have prepared the reader for his next book.

4. WRITING RADNORSHIRE

With his third book, Bruce Chatwin sprang a surprise. Established as a chronicler of extraordinary events in extraordinary places he published, in 1982, a book about two Welsh hill farmers whose lives could only be seen as mundane in comparison with the characters he had drawn in Patagonia or Dahomey. He explained himself in an interview with Michael Ignatieff:

> It always irritated me to be called a travel writer. So I decided to write something about people who never went out. That's how On The Black Hill came into being. (*Granta*, p.27)

There is perhaps more to the genesis of the book than this. Chatwin's involvement with the Welsh border country dated back, as has been discussed earlier, to a childhood trip with his father. His next visit was from Marlborough as part of a youth club summer camp that had the aim of mixing the social classes through activities such as walling and roofing. Later, he stayed at Llanthony Abbey, once owned by Walter Savage Landor and now a hotel but, at the time Chatwin stayed, occupied by an Italian contessa who set up her table in the cloister like a nineteenth century landlord to receive rents from her tenants. He told the poet Hugo Williams: "Hardly anything has changed around here since my grandparents came on bicycling tours as teenagers. Even the clothes are the same. You can still get the double-fronted striped shirts in Hay-on-Wye." In an interview given to Melvyn Bragg on London Weekend Television's *South Bank Show*, Chatwin said that he had often thought of the landscape of the Welsh borders, of the Black Mountains and the Radnor Forest, "as if it were my home in many ways". He had

come there as a child "and it's my home base, a sort of metaphorical home base if you like and it's the place I love".

Chatwin had friends in the area: he stayed regularly with
Penelope Chetwode (Lady Betjeman) another adventurous
traveller who lived above Hay, and with Diana Melly at her
thirteenth century Norman watchtower near Brecon where
much of the book was eventually written. He stayed, too,
with an old friend, Martin Wilkinson, near Clun where the
book was begun. It was at Lady Betjeman's table that he was
introduced to some of the more prominent members of Hay
society like the bookseller Richard Booth, the self-styled
'King of Hay'. Booth found the writer too much of an intellectual for his taste, and accuses him now of taking a romantic
view of the people of the Black Mountains. "I felt very
strongly that he was taking an intellectual's view of it," he
says, "without realising how the local economy works, how it
did still continue." Booth is unimpressed by the fact that most
local people loved the book and found it a fair reflection of
the Radnorshire reality. "These people are too inclined to go
down well locally," he observes tartly.

Ros Fry, who worked at the Blue Boar in Hay, recalls that
Chatwin frequently came in for lunch: "He was always watch-
ing people, how they spoke, and their mannerisms." He was
also able to efface himself in the interests of observation and
recording ("No-one really knew him") but when he wished to
he could shine: "He had quite a theatrical way about him if he
wanted to. He had a face that you really wanted to look at. His
eyes really glittered. If he had been born in the twelfth century
he would have been a wizard." Chatwin insisted that Rhulen in
the book could have been any one of the border towns (he men-
tions specifically Kington or Knighton) but it would be unwise
to suggest that to the citizens of Hay. Certainly, an identification of the topography of the novel with the Llanthony valley
seems reasonable enough, although Chatwin was drawing on
explorations and researches up and down the border, even as
far north as Clun.

A typical local reader of *On The Black Hill* was Mrs Nancy
Powell who lives at a hill farm near Hay and who read the book
with great eagemess, recognising many of the stories in it. The
shooting at Lower Brechfa, for example was based on a real

incident, thought to have happened in 1926. Certainly the *Hereford Times* for that year records two very similar incidents. In May 1926 a man called Godfrey Thomas, who lived with his aged mother at Henllys Farm, Tregare, near Raglan in Monmouthshire, attempted to shoot Alice Powell of Ty Pwll Farm, Tregare, following a lovers' quarrel and then shot himself dead with the same shotgun. In September, also near Raglan, Albert Rudge, a farm-worker, shot dead 19-year-old Doris Moody at her home, Pentre Cottage, Llandenny. In spite of shooting himself and then trying to drown in the village pond, Albert was brought before Monmouth magistrates with his arm in a sling, looking, understandably, "ill and haggard". At the assizes his love letter to the girl, which was also a suicide note, was read out. She had apparently returned his engagement ring by post. Rudge was found guilty but detained as criminally insane "until His Majesty's pleasure be known". The inquest jury at Monmouth Assizes was so moved by the girl's mother's plight that they handed her their fees.

Mrs Powell also recalls many cases of twins who would not marry for fear of losing part of the farm to the other's widow. And she remembers a well-known case of a vicar's daughter, like Mary Jones, who ran off with a carpenter and had two bachelor sons who farmed together until the 1960s when a divorcee "managed to prise them apart" by marrying one of them. For Mrs Powell the book was "very convincing, very good on farm life". She adds: "He painted a wonderful picture of my mother's day and age." Pressed on whether there was any element of condescension in the book, a frequent charge levelled at those who write from outside a community, she replies simply: "He had no bones to pick with the people".

Local readers were also more likely to seize with delighted recognition on very minor details. Mrs Mary Lewis, landlady of the Bull's Head at Craswall, was struck by the reference to the gathering up of stray sheep into the paddock adjacent to the Shepherd's Rest pub:

> From seven in the morning, farmers on horseback had been clearing the hill, and the bleating white mass was now safe in Evan Bevan's paddock, waiting to be sorted after lunch. (*On The Black Hill*, p.176)

"The sheep stray place was here," she says, "It's still held here on the second Saturday in July." If there was a real life model for the Shepherd's Rest in the book, then it would certainly be the Bull's Head. Mrs Lewis remembers Chatwin coming in to the tiny inn with Lady Betjeman, although she had no idea at that time that he was writing a book set in the area. Like Mrs Powell she greatly enjoyed the book and thought it was a fair portrait: "I didn't see nothing wrong with it." She also recognised some of the stories: "You could place people in it."

On The Black Hill, however, is not a work of social anthropology but a novel. The intensive research that Chatwin carried out in writing it should not disguise the fact that it is "a work of the imagination". Whatever the documentary sources or echoes it is an imaginative reordering of experience. It would be fruitless to try and pursue a form of literary sleuthing that tried to find the original of every character and the source of every incident. The twins, for example, appear to have been suggested by real life originals but Chatwin insisted that Benjamin and Lewis were an amalgam of at least three sets of twins. Equally, the place names used in the book could confuse the literal-minded. There is a Rhulen on the Ordnance Survey map and there is a Vision farmhouse but these were raided for their names only and are not the ones in the book. Sometimes the playful reordering and random borrowing is obvious, as when a character appears called Mr Evenjobb, the name of a village in the Radnor Valley.

According to Hugo Williams, Chatwin spoke to many Radnorshire men who had survived the First World War and described how one of them was so shocked by the sight of the raised hemlines of the twenties on one of his rare visits to town that he turned back, physically sick. "It was this shock of light from another era that was to become the theme of Chatwin's book," Williams maintained, "the theme of a century turning back in horror from what it was approaching. By the time he had written thirty pages describing this cataclysmic confrontation of men and women, represented by the nineteenth and twentieth centuries, he realised he was onto something more than just a short story." On the *South Bank Show*, he described this in more detail:

> I was told a story, it doesn't matter which one, which does appear in the book, about two bachelor brothers, and I wanted to write a short story. And so I started out writing a few paragraphs and then, suddenly, I wrote that the brothers were identical twins. I don't know why I wrote it, but it just occurred to me that they might be. And having written that line, which is a separate paragraph to itself, I suddenly realised that this was a novel and not a short story and that what I'd done sort of predicated a book of 450 pages instead of 30. And so one just had to carry on till the end.

This account of the genesis of the book differs from the one he gave Ignatieff in the interview quoted above, making it seem much more random a choice of subject. Perhaps Chatwin himself was unable to pinpoint the moment at which the book began to coalesce as an idea in his mind and his real reasons for choosing both location and theme may have been more complex than these accounts given spontaneously in interviews.

In this interview Chatwin was a little more specific about the geographical particularity of the novel's setting. "The areas that I know," he told Bragg, "are the Black Mountains and the Radnor Forest. It can in fact happen anywhere between South Shropshire and Monmouthshire, in theory, because it's all the same board and it's all got the same character." He also gave the first of several insights into the working methods of what the novelist John Updike was later to term in his *New Yorker* review of the book "the demon researcher". Chatwin said that he did the research as he went along. He appears to have had a very clear idea about what he wanted in advance but he was equally open to accidental discovery: "As you're trying to find it, something else happens which leads you to another story which you may or may not put in." He compared the process to an enormous jigsaw puzzle of interlocking facts. He admitted that some characters went straight into the book from real life "but I've done the usual novelist thing of combining two, three, four characters and then the character has a life of his own". He was frank about his methods:

> It has the same tenuous dividing line between fact and fiction and real people and something invented. And I quite honestly used them. If you're off on a journey, you meet somebody, they go into the book in one form or another. (*South Bank Show*)

He never made notes during an interview but "just occasion-ally" — as he came away from a farmhouse — he would jot down something someone had said. He would then check what he had been told against newspaper reports. He went to the public library at Hereford and turned the enormous pages of the bound copies of *The Hereford Times*, fascinated by the detail. Many of the reports, he told Bragg, "read like short stories themselves. The standard of reporting is incredible." Hugo Wil-liams says he would sometimes go back to his original inform-ant, armed with more precise information and dates from *The Hereford Times*, which would then generate more (and often more concrete) information. Another of his research techniques, which he explained to Charles Way, the dramatist who adapted the book for the Made in Wales Theatre Company, was to ap-proach farmers, carrying a particular book, *Welsh Rural Life in Photographs* by Elfyn Scausfield, and point to a picture as a means of provoking a reflection or a shaft of recognition.

While staying near Brecon with Diana Melly Chatwin met a local farmer at Llanfrynach, Simon Harpur, who was to become an invaluable source of information about Radnorshire farming life and traditions. Simon Harpur's family had farmed locally for generations, and in a very traditional way, and he was able to produce records from the turn of the century which answered Chatwin's many questions about, say, the price of corn in 1910 or how much the stallion man would charge. This character in the book, Merlin Evans, who tours the borders with his stallion, Spanker, and who, according to legend, sires more illegitimate children than foals, was modelled on a real figure who used to walk his stallion around the farms until the last war. Today in Radnorshire farmers put their mare more prosai-cally in a horse box and drive it to the stallion. "It was always a high spot in the year when the stallion man came round," Simon Harpur explains. He was acknowledged as a local char-acter and many stories were told about him. Harpur praises Chatwin's skill in taking these stories and weaving convincing patterns out of them: "He created an atmosphere wonderfully well. He really does capture the essence of it because it is very much in the vein of living in a country district. This looseness of reality is part of the stories country people tell. The real stallion man was probably as dull as the mechanic who mends the car."

1. Bruce Chatwin

2. The Broad and Narrow Path

3. The Vision farmhouse, from the film

4. Amos and Mary Jones, from the film

5 & 6. Brothers in bed, from the film and stage play

7. Brothers together, from the stage play

8. Eightieth birthdays at the airfield, from the film

9 & 10. The hard farming life, from the film and stage play

11 & 12. A visit to the Welsh borders by the stage cast

13 & 14. Historical farm life: reaping in Powys, 1918, and a Dyfed hay
   harvest in the 1930s

The additions and embellishments of oral tradition were part of the way that local people perceived reality and Chatwin's narrative method was not dissimilar. Inevitably he was selective, and perhaps the memories of his local readers were also selective, screening out the really bad times. Simon Harpur thinks that in some ways "he didn't get close to the bone" but this is no criticism: "He has the flavour." Part of the reason for his success was that he was "a very, very good listener. He was incredibly attentive to what other people had to say. He gave a lot of thought and consideration to what people did say." If Simon Harpur has any reservation about the book it is perhaps with the Theo-Meg relationship which he is unconvinced by and sees as an attempt by Chatwin to place himself in the book and "fabricate a bond" between a thoughtful outsider and a local woman that would in reality have taken years to evolve.

In his recorded comments Chatwin seems to imply that the emergence of the theme of twins was almost an accident (which did not stop one ingenious critic purporting to discover the word encoded in Chatwin's own surname) but once the the the idea emerged he was off on the research trail to the British Museum where he examined all the psychoanalytic literature on twins "but that didn't seem to me to be very interesting". He then tried a work on twins by the French scholar Professor Zazo which contained a selection of some of the 1500 case studies the scholar had examined. "Each one was a tiny little short story," said Chatwin. He decided to pay a call on the elderly professor, whom he told about the projected novel, explaining that he had used many of his case histories in it. Would you mind, asked the writer, if I tell you the story of my twins, letting me know whether I have gone wrong? "Of course not, Sir" replied the professor, "If I had your talents I could be Balzac." He listened to the projected story of Benjamin and Lewis and made various suggestions. Chatwin told Melvyn Bragg: "that really became the structure of the book".

According to Hugo Williams, Chatwin had started work on what was to become *On The Black Hill* before he had completed *The Viceroy of Ouidah*. He put it aside to complete the earlier novel and shortly afterwards discovered the American writer's colony, Yaddo. From Yaddo he wrote to an old friend, Diana Melly, saying he had an idea for a book and asking if he could come and stay at her house in the Usk valley to write it. In fact, he had written part of it already while staying earlier at the home of another friend, Martin Wilkinson, who lived at Clunton in South Shropshire. He spent several weeks at Clunton in October and November 1980 and worked in a light, airy room in a converted flat over the stable block. Over his work-station he pinned a reproduction of *The Broad and Narrow Path*, the religious colour print that in the novel hung in The Vision farm in a frame carved by Amos Jones. The simplicity and austerity of the nonconformist chapel culture fascinated Chatwin and he would often pay visits to a chapel at Hay-on-Wye during his researches. He worked hard, often until nine o'clock in the evening (but always with walks during the day). Martin Wilkinson recalls how he would come and read passages to him and was often "terribly elated" if he felt that a particular day's writing had gone well.

A few yards from the house there is a gate to a path which climbs up the hill, past the rusted skeleton of an old Ford sinking into mud and nettles. Passing through a second gate, the walker comes on a simple wooden Forestry Commission sign which reads: BLACK HILL. Chatwin returned from one of his walks, Martin Wilkinson recalls, brimming with excitement and declaring: "I've found my title!" In terms of the landscape of the book, however, this particular Black Hill (there is more than one on the Ordnance Survey map) would not quite fit and it is best to see it as Chatwin once again raiding the map for a title and constructing his own imaginary topography. This hill, before being clothed in conifer plantation, was open moorland and Chatwin enjoyed hearing from neighbours about the experiences of whinberry-pickers. This tiny blue berry growing on the hills and sometimes known in Radnorshire as wimberry (it is in fact the bilberry or whortleberry), although eatable, was also in demand for use as dye. Picking the tiny berries is hard work (a form of wooden comb was often used) and the local people, who worked on piece rates for Birmingham dealers, were once so enraged by the tyrannical behaviour of one of their bosses that they stripped him and rolled him in a tub of bilberries.

According to Martin Wilkinson, Chatwin saw himself as a dispassionate observer who was only just beginning to bring his own feelings into his work with *Utz* "He was very wary of his own emotions." He admired fastidious observers and literary craftsmen like Flaubert. "He applied the same technique to his emotions." He was also fond of saying that the writer was a "cutpurse", a raider of other people's experiences. At the same time he was a very vital companion who could exhibit "terrific bonhomie and charm" and although generally quieter and more reserved than he is sometimes represented as being, could, when he chose to be, turn into an amusing "playful, bragging figure" who enjoyed playing the role implicit in his old Sotheby's nickname 'Chatwina', camping it up for the amusement of his friends. "But the real Bruce was very direct and sincere. He didn't waste words."

Martin Wilkinson also confirms Chatwin's tangential relationship to English culture. "His outlook was transatlantic. He was married to an American and he had spent a lot of time in New York. The English cultural establishment turned him off." His days at Sotheby's, too, seem to have implanted a deep dislike of certain sections of English society. And his loathing for the chairman of Sotheby's, Peter Wilson, appears to have stayed cordial, although his love of art was always "powerful".

After writing the first part of the novel in Shropshire Chatwin was to write the bulk of the book while staying with Diana Melly, working very regularly as he had in Clunton and starting at eight in the morning at the typewriter. He always wrote his first drafts in longhand on yellow legal pads and had a fogeyish distrust of the wordprocessor, claiming to be able to spot any novel written using one. He remained in the habit of reading his work aloud as it was composed. In the evenings, says Diana Melly, "He read what he had written that day to me to make sure it was smooth." Sometimes Francis Wyndham was in the audience, too, since he and Diana Melly were collaborating at the time on an edition of the letters of Jean Rhys. Sometimes, when he was particularly pleased with a passage, Chatwin would bound down the stairs in the middle of the day to read it out while it was fresh.

On The Black Hill begins with an epigraph from the seventeenth century divine Jeremy Taylor, whose prose style Chatwin had long admired. It concerns the transitoriness of human existence and enjoins that "we must look somewhere else for an abiding city". It introduces both the theme of the novel — that we can "fix oure house" only in "another countrey" and that there is no prospect of utopia in this life — and the book's religious undertow. The critic Karl Miller called *On The Black Hill* "a Christian romance", noting the significance of the titles of the farms ('The Vision', 'The Rock') and the landscape with its "holy innocents, ragged saints, Franciscan animal lovers". Meg, who is like some Celtic wood-spirit, and Theo — the name is of evident significance — embody the book's essential message, a countervailing anti-materialism or ascetic spirituality to be set against the acquisitiveness, cupidity, and jealousy ("the sins of settlement") of so many of the denizens of the Black Hill. The twins, who in their gentle, dim, trusting way, take a shine to Theo and pay him an awkward but polite visit in his tent or hermit's lair, glimpse some of this but it is too late for them to shake off their material ties. The book's climactic image — the aeroplane flight — is their symbolic moment of escape from a claustrophobic and terrestrial existence. For the most part they are anchored to The Vision, an ironic term for a place so circumscribed and harshly quotidian.

Chatwin was obsessed with the Biblical story of Cain and Abel which he saw as a fundamental paradigm of the nomad and the settler, of the two great human impulses that were in conflict: to settle and acquire the habits of civilisation, and to wander. He said that "one of the most interesting questions that has ever been posed by any work of literature" was why Abel (whose hands, after all were red with blood sacrifice) was the martyr and Cain, the settled agriculturalist (and by implication, thought Chatwin, a vegetarian), was the killer. This became easier to understand, he argued, once you realised that the word Abel means motion, transitoriness, breath, and therefore life, whereas the word Cain comes from a verbal root, meaning to accumulate and acquire, making the agriculturalist a property owner. He expounded all this enthusiastically to Melvyn Bragg:

> Once you get these two things in opposition, you start to realise that the whole of the Bible is this fantastic drama, a great dilemma in which the arguments are going back and forth as to whether it is right to settle or whether it is right to move, and Jehovah never really quite decides definitely. God, in other words — perhaps instinct — is on the side of the Nomads. (*South Bank Show*)

The characters in the novel are religious in a more straightforward sense too. In late nineteenth and early twentieth century Radnorshire church and chapel played a fundamental part in the life of the population. Not only do Mary and Amos Jones first notice each other at a Church service, but institutionalised religion, and its various pastors, are key players in the book. The engraving of 'The Broad and Narrow Path' which hangs in The Vision highlights the way that religion, and class, threaded their way into the landscape. The picture shows the "ladies and gentlemen" languidly strolling towards perdition and engaged in various ungodly pursuits, while the righteous walk firmly towards salvation through a landscape visibly that of Welsh nonconformity, reminding the twins, as they gazed on the picture, of "an illustrated brochure for Llandrindod Wells". The image haunts Benjamin's imagination to the extent that he believed seriously that "the road to Hell was the road to Hereford, whereas the road to Heaven led up to the Radnor Hills". Chatwin admired the nonconformist chapels which he said were like the original Christian communities and he linked their plainness and lack of ceremony to his belief in the necessity of asceticism. "I've always thought that some kind of ritual is an essential ingredient of human life," he said, "and I think that the essential religious services should have this austere quality." Towards the end of his life, however, he was drawn to the more ornate and hieratic ceremonial of the Greek Orthodox church.

On The Black Hill immediately signals its affinity with the tradition of the rural novel in English and calls to mind the world of Hardy or George Eliot as well as more immediately obvious local precursors such as Mary Webb or Francis Kilvert. The first meeting of Mary and Amos Jones in Rhulen church has an echo of Hardy's poem 'A Church Romance (Mellstock: *circa* 1835)' where Amos' baritone performs the function of the "strenuous viol" in Hardy's poem. The opening description of The Vision farmhouse ("The border of Radnor and Hereford was said to run right through the middle of the staircase") echoes Kilvert's diary entry for Friday 18 November 1870 where he feels for the boundary notch in a chimney and remembers the story of another house, the Pant at Brilley, where the midwife is said to have delivered a child standing up so that it could be born in the corner of the room that was in England. Chatwin's opening descriptions of the farmhouse and its interior display his eidetic gift for vivid realisation of object and place. Steeped as he was in the literary associations of what he described, he was also a keen observer of present actuality. The picture of the farmhouse, drawn in a few sentences, seems exactly right and farms like it ("roughcast walls and a roof of mossy stone tiles...at the far end of the farmyard in the shade of an old Scots pine...an orchard of wind-stunted apple trees") can be seen all over Radnorshire today.

Like *The Viceroy of Ouidah*, the book begins in the present, as the twins, Benjamin and Lewis Jones, prepare to hand over the farm to their nephew Kevin. It then starts to go back in time to tell a story, roughly contemporary to the twentieth century itself, in the familiar short sections — fifty in all — which had been the structural feature of his two earlier books. The framework of immobility and fixed custom is established — even their clothes show the marks of repeated habit: like Lewis's hat whose peak has lost its nap as a result of his lifting it to every stranger. The house is like a museum to the memory of their mother. They have deliberately opted for stasis, for trying to resist time. And, lest anyone see this as an incipient rural idyll, there is the hint of inadequacy and sexual dysfunction. The sole creative pursuit of their father — carving picture frames — had been the occasion of the "meanness" going briefly out of him that was otherwise his natural condition. They are physically constrained by never having gone further than Hereford apart from one seaside holiday. These restricted horizons merely "inflamed Lewis's passion for geography". Neither of the twins has married and Benjamin has assumed the domestic 'feminine' roles of cooking and cleaning and is the 'wife' of this sexless 'marriage' whose partners sleep side by side in their mother's bed. The novel will later develop this sense of thwarted sexuality which drives Lewis to seek sexual experience outside the farm in a way which fills Benjamin with jealous anger. So intense is this sexual jealousy that it is often registered paranormally. Their final deprivation is their sterility, their absence of an heir. Young Kevin fulfils this role, however, and the terms of relief in which his appearance is greeted only confirm the backlog of damage and inadequacy in their lives. When they saw him: "they knew that their lives had not been wasted and that time, in its healing circle, had wiped away the pain and the anger, the shame and the sterility, and had broken into the future with the promise of new things" (p.14).

Pain, anger, shame and sterility are also the lot of their father, Amos, in his first marriage whose ending with the death of his wife drives him to religion. The arrival of Mary Latimer, the vicar's daughter, promises some alternative to the bitterness and lack of possibility which seems Amos's lot and for which the gloomy sermons of Jeremy Taylor ("As our life is very short, so it is very miserable") would seem to furnish the appropriate text. In spite of the class and cultural differences between them — the first act of violence towards his new wife is to prove to be the hurling into her eye of a copy of *Wuthering Heights* — their attraction is immediate, if not entirely explicable. It has a clear physical element and is suggestive of deep if inarticulate feeling. Almost immediately on seeing Amos, Mary "felt her heart was breaking" and when he learns of her father's death "he saw that his hand was shaking". But when they meet, they have nothing to say and "creep back to their shells". His new love opens up for Amos a small window of possibility: "He felt light-hearted, almost happy, as if his life, too, would begin afresh." Even at the threshold of expectation, however, he can manage to be only "almost happy". Their relationship develops against the backcloth of the Black Hill which Chatwin evokes in the simplest and most direct language: "Two buzzards were wheeling and falling in the blue air, and there were lambs and crows in a bright green field" (p.19). These notations have something of the plain, elemental force of epic. Eventually, Amos and Mary are driven together by a recognition of mutual need: Amos needs a wife, a farm, and sons to inherit it, Mary needs to escape dependency on relatives or having to go into service. Once the decision is made, she puts aside her natural delicacy and squeamishness and reveals a new determination. When the Vision farm comes up for rent it is she who declares firmly: "Winter is coming. We have no time to lose."

If the "peasants", as the local land agent describes them, are constricted, the upper classes in the novel are, for their part, equally constrained. Mary's visit to Lurkenhope to plead for the lease on the farm (she will play the class card again later in the

novel) is the opportunity to glimpse the decadence of the Bickertons, an old Catholic family made rich by the West India
trade. Mrs Bickerton is tolerable because she is an artist and
married the Colonel "possibly to annoy her artist friends" —
Chatwin was always sympathetic to bourgeois iconoclasm —
but the younger generation whose "moneyed laughter" echoes
around the fake castle are not intended to endear. Offered a last
chance to join the élite as a governess and to avoid the judgement of her sister in Cheltenham who thinks the marriage "beneath you", Mary declines. Even the sympathetic Mrs Bickerton
exhibits a blithe lack of understanding. "I like the Welsh," she
tells Mary, "but they do seem to get angry, later."

Not that Mary abandons her breeding entirely. The farmhouse
becomes the location of unaccustomed genteel tea parties and
its presiding influence is Mrs Beeton. But after first treating his
wife as "a fragile object that had come by chance into his pos-
session and might easily break in his hands", Amos (influenced
by his cantankerous mother, Hannah Jones) realises that his fel-
low-farmers may be mocking his wife's pretensions and loses
patience with her refinement. The final straw is a mild Indian
curry, hurled to the floor as "filthy Indian food", which is the
occasion of their first marital conflict. Amos internalises his
anger, roaring "I won't hit you", and goes out on walkabout,
sleeping rough, and avoiding the farm. By the end of the winter,
Mary has begun to take the measure of her condition:

> There were days when it occurred to her that she had sat for years
> in the same damp, dark room, in the same trap, living with the same
> bad-tempered man...she began to identify herself with the one,
> wind-battered thorn-bush that she could see from her window. (*On
> The Black Hill*, p.35)

There is perhaps an echo here, in the image of "the one wind-
battered thorn bush", of R.S. Thomas's poem 'Evans' in his collection, *Poetry for Supper*. In that poem the narrator comes into a
bleak farmhouse interior ("his stark farm on the hill ridge") and
finds "the drip/Of rain like blood from the one tree/Weather-
tortured" less appalling than "the dark/Silting the veins of that
sick man/I left stranded upon the vast/And lonely shore of his
bleak bed". Another poem in that collection, 'Meet the Family',
might suggest some line of filiation to the Jones family. Cer-

tainly, R.S. Thomas, with his unsparing vision of life in "the bald Welsh hills" is exploring a similar terrain to Chatwin but, so far at least, there is no evidence that the latter read R.S. Thomas. In spite of his love for the Welsh borders he gives no hint, in his writing or in published interviews, of any intimacy with the literature of Wales, past or present, preferring always to talk of his beloved Russian writers. The lines of poetry put into the mouth of Theo the Tent are from Li Po not from any contemporary Welsh or English writer.

The coming of spring weather ends Amos's seasonal discontent ("Be the winter as makes me mad") and Mary's pregnancy seals the reconciliation. If Hannah Jones is a baleful, premonitory presence, her husband Sam the Waggon's gaiety — he has "run about the world" — lightens the atmosphere until the twins are born. The twins, Benjamin and Lewis, form an immediate bond with each other and with their mother which excludes Amos. Identical as they are, individual characteristics start to emerge. When Benjamin, the weaker of the two, is stung by a wasp it is Lewis who whimpers with pain. "This was the first time Lewis demonstrated his power to draw the pain from his brother, and take it on himself." They evolve a secret language and share everything, even splitting their sandwiches in two. Sam takes them on "the English walk" down to the lush fields around Lurkenhope or "the Welsh walk" up past The Rock, where Aggie and Tom Watkins live, towards the Radnor Hills "their humped outlines receding grey on grey towards the end of the world". Sam teaches them the names of the hills of the Radnor Forest: the Whimble, the Bach, the Black Mixen and the Smatcher. He also teaches them the Welsh for "dirty Saxon" after a spat on the path with the effete young Reggie Bickerton. This suppressed Welsh nationalist theme recurs fitfully in the novel: at the army recruitment meeting, at the auction of farms, and when a drunken Welshman is beaten up on the station platform when the twins set off for their holiday at St David's. The Welsh, in these instances, are powerless and at a disadvantage, incapacitated by drunkenness or anger. There is never a sense of constructive resistance to "the Dirty Saxon".

The shortcomings of the life of a hill-farmer's wife start to weigh heavily on Mary. She confides in the vicar, the Reverend Thomas Tuke, an arrogant classical scholar and huntsman who takes special pleasure in little acts which outrage the villagers whom he terms contemptuously "drones". Mary nonetheless likes his "sense of the ridiculous" and his sharp turn of phrase and he arranges for the twins to be properly educated — much to the disgust of Amos who is angered less by education itself than by its likely consequence of making the twins want to leave the farm. Mary confesses to the Rev Tuke that "farm life depressed her; that she was starved of conversation and ideas". Looking at her children after the funeral of Sam she notes "how thin and tired they were", measuring the cost of this life on them. Amos becomes violent and the feuds with neighbours at The Rock intensify his gloom. After the Watkins' act of arson Mary looks at her husband's eyes which "once friendly, sank in their sockets and peered, as if down a tunnel, at a hostile world outside". He is tormented by his "demons" and soon it leads him towards religious fanaticism. Abandoning the church he takes up with the chapel when a new minister Owen Gomer Davies arrives from North Wales. Mary's prejudices against nonconformity — the word chapel to her "represented all that was harsh and cramped and intolerant" — take some time to defeat. Even with his new zeal the ranting and raving of Amos does not stop and "Mary saw no end to the misery. She wanted to die, but knew she had to live for the twins".

The twins soon begin to display their oddities of character. After a dangerous childhood illness Benjamin becomes obsessed with death and one day Mary catches him dressing up in her clothes, having daubed himself in cologne. Benjamin starts to cook and to control the pair's money while Lewis begins to develop his interest in flight and starts a scrapbook that would eventually be devoted to air disasters. Although they are prone to mistake their reflection in the mirror for their other half, the twins develop quite separate personalities. Lewis is interested in girls and in foreign places while Benjamin "never thought of abroad" and regards the opposite sex with horror. He is, however, very fond of sheep and is very religious. Mary sometimes watches the two of them and senses that "one day they would both slide back into the old, familiar patterns of dependence". Always, she is haunted by a sense of entrapment.

The Great War is the first major historical event to have an impact on their lives. Some critics have suggested that there is something perfunctory and schematic about the historical framework of the novel. Professor Dai Smith of the University of Wales at Cardiff, who chaired a discussion on the book at the 1991 Hay-on-Wye Festival of Literature, said later: "I suppose my feeling was that Chatwin had written a kind of pastoral in which the outside world flitted by but the twins were not properly affected by it. Granted that he wished to show their lives as separated, distanced even, but, then, his manner of representing the other world creaked along on 'significant' dates and newspaper headlines." The War is announced in the book, for example, by a man calling over the hedge to say the Germans had marched into Belgium. It was certainly Chatwin's intention to show how the occupants of The Vision were at a tangent to history and perhaps this cartoon-strip historical diorama that stands in for direct experience of twentieth century history is appropriate to the immature and sheltered perceptions of the twins who see no reason to accept any responsibility for events outside their own immediate experience.

The War takes Lewis away from the farm, and from Benjamin who reacts strangely to the separation: "He hated Lewis for leaving and suspected him of stealing his soul." Both young men have a bizarre faculty of communicating over distances which may stretch some readers' credulity but which presumably found some sanction in Chatwin's researches into the literature of twins or in the learned opinion of Professor Zazo. When biting into a pasty in a Hereford cafe Lewis suddenly starts to exhibit sympathetic symptoms of shivering and knows by this sign that his brother is in danger. Benjamin is lost in the snow and Lewis, sensing this, runs to the station. Arriving at The Vision after four o'clock he is told by his sister that the rest of the family have gone out to look for Benjamin. He replies simply: "And I know where him do be." After Benjamin's eventual rescue he regains consciousness and accuses Lewis: "You left me." Again, when Benjamin is forced by the war tribunal to accept call-up, Lewis feels the physical maltreatment meted out to Benjamin at the barracks although he is many miles away. The intensity of this relationship is felt as a shackle by Lewis but not by Benjamin. It is the restless man, the thwarted wanderer, who suffers.

Chatwin's presentation of the victory parade at the National

Peace Celebrations at Lurkenhope Park exhibits a strong under-tone of dislike for militarism. The stilted, dead language of the canting members of the local establishment with their rhetoric about other people's sufferings shows them hopelessly out of touch with their audience. But in general Chatwin is less good with his upper class characters — who frequently tend towards caricature — than with his more ordinary protagonists. Reggie Bickerton, disabled by the war but still chasing after the female servants, is a case in point. Yet the fortunes of The Vision are linked to those of the Bickertons, whose post-war decline, whilst giving Amos the opportunity for "moralistic sermons on the decline of the gentry", results in the sale of the farms to the tenants and further distress for Amos. The feudal power rela-tions of Radnorshire society are not disguised.

For the twins, the War was their opportunity to connect with the outside world and they turned it down: "Since the day of the peace celebrations, the twins' world had contracted to a few square miles." Deliberately, they turned away from the modern age represented by modern farm machinery. Mary is worried by this: "Already, though only twenty two, her sons were be-having like crabby old bachelors." Their father, meanwhile, is finally broken by the retribution meted out to him at the auction by Tom Watkins. His old enemy alone breaks the agreement that no farmer bid against an existing tenant. After this defeat Amos retreats into himself. He resents Mary's ability to salvage the situation by once again using her class connections, and he tries to shift the blame onto her for sending away his daughter Rebecca when she became pregnant.

Mary's appeal to Mrs Bickerton, over the head of the land agent who accuses her of having "betrayed her class", results in a letter from the south of France. A mimosa flower falls from the envelope and Mary catches momentarily "the smell of the South" and is reminded sharply of the extent of her deprivation. That scent is also:

> a sentence to stay, trapped for ever and for ever, for the rest of her existence in this gloomy house below the hill. (*On The Black Hill*, p.146)

After the death of Amos, she begins to turn back from time

and the house turns slowly into a museum. She makes one last attempt to get the twins married by packing them off to Rhulen fair but Benjamin returns, horrified by the short skirts and the exposed legs which remind him of a visit to the abbatoir and "the kicks of the sheep in their death throes". And perhaps she was not even serious herself, for that night she brushes her cheek against Benjamin's on the stair "and, with a sly smile, thanked him for bringing his brother home". Abandoning any idea that they will leave, she buys them bicycles for their thirty-first birthday and they develop an interest in mediaevalism and the Celtic saints. In the year that the slump was biting in the South Wales valleys: "They considered taking up the life of anchorites."

Lewis's suppressed sexual desires, however, start to reassert themselves. His first attempt at seducing Mrs Musker is thwarted by Haines of Red Daren. The melodramatic events at Lower Brechfa, where Haines shoots Mrs Musker and then himself were, as noted above, actually based on newspaper reports of real events which are still remembered in the locality. Lewis's sexual pursuit is an index of his wider exclusion from normal human desires and experiences. He feels excluded, too, by Mary and Benjamin who do not take him into their confidence in business matters: "For some time the house had been troubled and divided. Lewis suspected both his mother and brother of conspiring against him: the fact that he was womanless was all part of their plan." His sexual salvation is eventually delivered by Joy Lambert, an artist of a type still frequent in the Welsh borders (Chatwin would undoubtedly have encountered such people) who, with her husband Nigel, "lived in terror of being considered middle class". They have a condescending fondness for the locals whom they dub the 'Earlies'. While Nigel comes to sketch the sheep shearers (in spite of Benjamin's distrust of anyone "from off") his wife, for a bet of a bottle of gin, finally seduces Lewis against a Scots pine. On his return home Mary and Benjamin know exactly what has happened and their reaction drives him away from The Vision to seek work on a pig farm at Weobley across the border in Herefordshire. Mary tries to mediate but recognises that it will be some time before Lewis can return because "Benjamin's love for Lewis was murderous". It is only when Mary dies that Lewis feels able to return. On the night of the funeral they enact a ritual of reconciliation to each other and to their fate. It is the night of their weekly bath and, after washing each other, they put on their father's nightshirts and go to their parents' bed. The fact that this is also the eve of the Second World War is of little relevance: "United at last by the memory of their mother, they forgot that all of Europe was in flames."

With the death of both parents the novel starts to enter its final phase, charting the post-war experiences of the solitary twins. The war, unsurprisingly, passed them by. The Battle of Britain was too big for Lewis's scrapbook and their only comment on the air raid on Coventry, seen as a dim glow on the distant horizon, is: "And a good job it isn't we". The dropping of the atomic bomb on Nagasaki, however, does appear to terrify them. Lewis makes one last attempt to reach tentatively out for some resolution of his private sense of loss when Lotte Zons arrives. She is a Viennese Jewish refugee and a Chatwinian investigator of twins whose researches are recorded in buckram-bound notebooks. Lewis confesses to her that "he'd always felt left out" and, as their friendship grows, he makes the final approach in his life to intimacy by trying to take her hand. "No," she says, " it would not be correct."

The twins then renew their relationship with Meg the Rock. In an interview Chatwin said that he consciously deployed a Celtic inspired imagery to describe the seasonal cycles and to give the book what he called "a kind of moral framework". If that is plausible, then Meg the Rock must be the principal piece of evidence. Chatwin told his interviewer:

> I find that the moment you move into Wales you suddenly have this curious reverence for nature among locals which is certainly enshrined in their language which you don't find much in England, and I think it's a tradition which goes back to the Celtic world. I think there is something which you could describe as the Celtic sensibility. (*South Bank Show*)

Meg is presented as a natural spirit who cannot read or write but who can mimic the voice of any animal or bird. The finches eat from her hand and one frosty morning she is seen, in her usual dress of five or six green jerseys, sitting on an upturned bucket "warming her hands around a mug of tea while the tits and chaffinches perched on her shoulder". Her nature-worship has a religious dimension: "When a green wood pecker took some crumbs from her hand, she imagined the bird was a messenger from God and sang His praises in doggerel all through the day." On another occasion the twins' newly discovered nephew Kevin is taken for a walk on which they stumble on Meg who is at first mistaken for a mossy-tree stump, green and surrounded by birds:

> Her skin was plastered with reddish mud. Her breeches were the colour of mud. Her hat was a rotting stump. And the tattered green jerseys, tacked one to the other, were the mosses, and creepers, and ferns. (*On The Black Hill*, p.210)

Her identification as a wood-spirit or dryad is complete.

Some critics of the book fastened on the character of Meg as an implausible or faintly ludicrous figure, who belonged more properly to the satirical world of Stella Gibbons' *Cold Comfort Farm*. The *Spectator* reviewer, Francis King, felt that it was difficult "not to feel uncomfortable when Meg the Rock is around". Others singled out Meg's account of the shooting of the starving pack of dogs at The Rock ("And the dogs was a-howlin' and a-yowlin'") as an example of a comic Starkadderish idiom. Yet, paradoxically, Chatwin was to stress that the character of Meg was based on an actual character with whom he is said to have kept in touch after the book was written. He also used some of her sayings when performing his reportedly perfect mimicry of the Radnorshire dialect and delighted listeners with his "a-howlin' and a-yowlin'". There is, perhaps, a wider problem here for critics who appear to have difficulty with attempts to reproduce rural speech patterns and who too easily invoke the spirit of *Cold Comfort Farm*. In the metropolitan centres, where literary judgements are made or validated, 'streetwise' speech patterns (in Cockney television dramas, for example) are invariably considered acceptable and plausible where their rural equivalents are judged risible. It is simply the case that even in the last decade of the twentieth century in Radnorshire certain speech patterns, dialectal variations, inversions of word order, and unusual vocabulary, persist in actual everyday speech. A builder in the Radnor Valley in the 1990s can still be found referring to a heap of building sand as a 'tump'.

Chatwin himself was very aware of the importance of authenticity and the avoidance of mockery in representing other people's ways of speaking. He told the playwright Charles Way that he had hurled a pocket radio against the wall in anger when the BBC adapted *In Patagonia* as a 'Book at Bedtime' and refused to listen to further instalments because of its "English-jokey South American" accents. He was apprehensive about the BBC's radio adaptation of *On The Black Hill* lest "they choose readers who are unaware of what a Welsh — and more particularly a Border accent is; they should be sat down for an hour or so in a pub in Hay-on-Wye and then they'd know for sure". In the end he scribbled an exasperated note to Way after hearing how the BBC planned to do it: "The BBC *would* want L and B's intimate thoughts — and how corny they must want them to be: the point being that the writer, if he is not brought up in that milieu, cannot write what he cannot know — or reasonably guess at. I don't envy you the task."

The representation of Meg was linked with that of Theo the Tent and the two together embody much of the meaning of the book. Theo, an exiled South African, is a gentle bear-like hippy who lives in a yurt on his own after falling out with a "cheap and tawdry" Eastern religious commune who milked him of his money. He is now a Taoist and pins his haikus to tree stumps on the Radnor hills. On his previous travels he has seen the Bushmen of the Kalahari: "And he had come to believe that all men were meant to be wanderers, like them, like St Francis." Sometimes he feels that even his simple shelter is "preventing him from following the Way". He is beguiled by Meg and sits for hours listening to "the harsh and earthy music of her voice" and feels that there is "something sacred about her rags". When the twins go and visit this man who has turned his back on the twentieth century in a different way from themselves, they see a shamanistic figure: "His hat was crowned with honeysuckle and he looked like Ancient Man." Theo reads to them from the eighth century Chinese poet Li Po, whom Chatwin was elsewhere to describe as "my favourite upland traveller". The author was fond, too, of the great Japanese poet and traveller Matsuo Basho, to whose *Narrow Road to the Deep North*, he introduced his friend Peter Levi. There is obviously much of Chatwin in the figure of Theo. The tolerance of the twins (in contemporary Radnorshire, landowners have formed a 'hippy watch' to prevent 'New Age Travellers' from camping on common land) is a deliberate strategy of Chatwin's to show how, earthbound as they are, they can recognise the independence of spirit and rejection of modern consumer-capitalism exhibited by Theo, even if they themselves could never follow the Way.

In spite of the manipulations of young Kevin's mother, Mrs Redpath, and the boy's manifest imperfections, he does provide a genuine sense of comfort to the emotionally undernourished old bachelors. Before his arrival, like their father and mother before them, they had begun to reflect on the grimness of their fate. The day of their sixtieth birthday, for example, was "almost a day of mourning" and gave them forebodings of a miserable old age:

> They would turn to the wall of family photos — row on row of smiling faces, all of them dead or gone. How was it possible, they wondered, that they had come to be alone? (*On The Black Hill*, p.203)

The day of their eightieth birthday is the climax of the book and the Cessna flight they make from what would plausibly be Shobdon airfield is a fairly unambiguous metaphor of escape from the eight decades of anchoring in one place. (It is also, in truth, a denouement disturbingly congruent with that of *Cold Comfort Farm* where an aeroplane flight performs a related function!) Lewis, the figure perhaps most damaged by the thwarting of so many of his aspirations and the shutting off of so much possibility, is free for a few moments at least:

> And suddenly he felt...that all the frustrations of his cramped and frugal life now counted for nothing, because, for ten magnificent minutes, he had done what he wanted to do. (*On The Black Hill*, p.240)

But soon they are back down to earth and the message of the preacher in the penultimate chapter at the Harvest Festival is more pertinent to their actual condition. In spite of Theo's magnificent reading of Revelations 21 ("And I saw a new heaven and a new earth") the New Jerusalem will not be seen in Radnorshire and the preacher, enfolding some of Jeremy Taylor's phrasing, reminds them that "the City we seek is an Abiding

City, a place in another country where we must find rest".

In November 1982 *On The Black Hill* was awarded the Whitbread Literary Award for best first novel (the judges evidently having decided that Chatwin's preceding "work of the imagination", *The Viceroy of Ouidah*, was not a novel) and the following spring it received the James Tait Black prize for best novel. It was an immediate critical success and attracted particular praise in the United States where it was seen as a very characteristic English rural novel. As *The New York Times Book Review* put it: "He belongs, like Lawrence and Hardy before him, to that line of novelists, poets, diarists and amateur naturalists who have made the rural life of Great Britain more intimately known to generations of readers than that of any other country in Europe or America." John Leonard in *The New York Times* wrote: "Thomas Hardy, as a poet and as novelist would have liked this book." In a long review in *The New Yorker* ('The Jones Boys') the novelist John Updike — who thought he was reviewing the writer's second novel — praised Chatwin's "clipped, lapidary prose that compresses worlds into pages". He observed that Chatwin wrote "in such short paragraphs that he seems to be constantly interrupting himself. His narratives must be savoured in short takes, like collections of short stories." He also liked the novelist's "mosaic of wonderfully sharp and knowing small scenes". Updike added to the comparison with Hardy by saying that the national peace celebrations at Lurkenhope "seem self-consciously to out-Flaubert, for satire and counterpoint, the agricultural fair in *Madame Bovary*". Admiring Chatwin's skill at mastering period detail and his "loving empathy into the inner lives such detail adorned", Updike worries at what this is all for. He sees the twins as the centrepiece "but there is something creepy here, and perhaps allegorical, that strains belief". He sees the central relationship as "a homosexual marriage" and in the end values the book for conveying a sense "of the immensity of time a human life spans, a span itself dwarfed by the perspectives of history". He is also awed by Chatwin's stylistic gifts: "His studied style — with something in it of Hemingway's chiselled bleakness, and something of Lawrence's inspired swiftness — touches on the epic."

Another critic, Andrew Sinclair in *The Times*, declared (mistakenly as it was to turn out) that the novel represented Chatwin's abandonment of foreign inspiration and signalled "the arrival of a major novelist who has come home to find his roots here, his truth in this soil". Francis King in *The Spectator* compared the novel's "claustrophobic world" with that of Mary Webb but found Chatwin "a better because more fastidious writer". He was also worried by certain passages (such as those featuring Meg and Theo) "when Mr Chatwin edges perilously near to the cliff edge of sentimentality and bathos". Anne Duchene in the *Times Literary Supplement* compared the "emblematic self-sufficiency" of the writing with that of David Garnett, not least because each writer pretends to be "a loyal slave of the accidental, while in fact he is magisterially pulling all the strings". V.S. Pritchett, in *The New York Review of Books*, observed that: "Strangeness plainly stated is the key to the book, the mingling of outward and inner life... He has perhaps learned from the Russians 'to make it strange'". Acknowledging the inevitable Hardy comparison, Pritchett pointed out that there was neither Hardy's "grand tragic plot" nor his "theatrical use of coincidence", and certainly no Victorian pessimism. Chatwin was also good at catching the feel of the life of the people: "He is not a professional sorrower at the toils of the peasantry."

Celebration rather than analysis has been the dominant mode of Chatwin criticism and it was only Karl Miller, in a review in *The London Review of Books*, who sounded a dissenting note. The review was expanded into a chapter of Miller's 1985 study of the imaginative literature of duality, *Doubles*, where the subject matter of *On The Black Hill* obviously deserved a place. Miller identified the writer's exotic country as "Chatwinshire" and said the book belonged to the literary category of the fairy tale of twins and the traveller's tale: "a mode of writing to which Mr Chatwin has always been drawn". Comparing "Chatwinshire" with Patagonia, Miller saw it as an exploration in Radnorshire of "the wonders of the near-at-hand". In a double-edged phrase, Miller describes Chatwin as "a gifted writer with access to an admiring public" and evidently has it in mind to take him down a peg or two. He mocks, oddly for a professor of English literature, the occasional exoticism of Chatwin's vocabulary, and fastens gleefully on Nancy Bickerton in the Rectory "yanking at some convolvulus that threatened to smother the phlox". Miller joins those who have seen the hand of *Cold Comfort Farm* in the book and adds a comparison with Flann O'Brien who also wrote of a world where "simpletons, saints and grotesques face a ubiquitous duplicity". In the end Miller is unconvinced by the book's basic thesis. "The country is better than the town, the novel seems to convey: but the country is terrible. Where, if not in heaven, are we to live?" He does not believe that its other-worldliness works and concludes: "This is a more accomplished and decorative book than it is an interesting one...which so far as it can be accounted Meg-magical or Theo-centric, fails". In a final gesture of high, dry Caledonian asperity he puts its success down to the fashionable concerns of contemporary readers:

> It appears, however, to have been well-received by sophisticated readers — by a readership which has lost its faith in God, but which has not lost its faith in literature, which is experiencing a world in many ways worse than it has been for a long time, and which has remained attentive to romantic religion, to anti-social romance, and to the charms of duality. (Miller, p.406)

When the book was adapted for stage and screen, however, it was once again a huge success. In 1986 the Made in Wales Theatre Company staged a version by Charles Way which was revived again in 1988 by Theatr Clwyd. Chatwin was generous to the project as he was to the film and wrote to Charles Way: "I can't see any objection to putting my two old twins on the stage" adding, "I can't for the life of me see how you'd do it: but that, of course, is your business." Chatwin paid a visit to the playwright at his home in Wales and Way recalls Chatwin arriving in dandyish mode, striding through the sober streets of Abergavenny in blue canvas sneakers "dressed like a surfer". He was eventually to catch up with the play on its second run in 1988 when the tour reached Waterman's Arts Centre in London. By then he was very ill with barely a year to live and a chair had to found for him in the foyer. He insisted on going backstage afterwards, however, to talk to the actors and he told those playing the twins, Sean Tudor-Owen and Andy Rivers, and Meg, Vivienne Moore, how much they had brought their originals back to him.

The novel became, in the 1980s, something of a cult book, enormously popular in the Welsh border region. Andrew

Grieve's film of *On The Black Hill*, starring Bob Peck and Gemma Jones and two Welsh actors, Mike and Robert Gwilym, as the twins, renewed the book's popularity, shooting the paperback version back into the bestseller lists.

The film was shot in seven weeks on location in March, April and May 1987 on a very tight budget of less than three quarters of a million pounds, achieved with the assistance of the British Film Institute. It used local people as extras (the director short-listed a hundred pairs of twins for audition) and the farm chosen to represent The Vision was near Sennybridge. It had been vacated only a year previously by a ninety-year-old woman and had no running water, just a spring in the back yard. Members of the woman's family advised the director on recreating its authenticity. Local craftsmen also offered advice and the popularity of the book locally meant that many local people came forward with offers of props. When Chatwin saw the choice for the farmhouse he joked to the director that it was more *echt* than anything he had in mind. In spite of the stunning photography by Thaddeus O'Sullivan and a largely faithful storyline, it omitted the "Meg-magical and Theo-centric" elements that had featured more prominently in the stage version. Andrew Grieve wrote that: "The problem of the passing years was overcome by concentration on the 'landmark' years of the twins' lives. By subtly aging them and by introducing the odd evocative prop — a car, a plane, a tractor or a hang-glider — it was possible to move the film through time without need for explanation. With a book of such richness there was always some detail that could be found to make a point or signal a change, and far from being a hindrance, the very complexity of the novel became an enormous help in writing the screenplay." The film opened in April 1988 at the Lumiere cinema in London and the Chapter cinema in Cardiff.

Chatwin had paid a flying visit to the set hot foot from Africa where Werner Herzog was filming *The Viceroy of Ouidah* as *Cobra Verde*. He was already suffering from the illness that would kill him within two years but according to Hugo Williams who saw him at this time he stopped all work on the set "talking, talking, talking to anyone who would listen, giggling at his own jokes, blue eyes gleaming out of his weatherbeaten, angelic face". A nativity play had been set up in Brecon for filming and when Chatwin saw it and heard the children speaking their lines he said: "That's exactly as I took it down. The intonations are exact." Andrew Grieve, like Charles Way, was struck by Chatwin's generosity and willingness to let the adaptors for stage and screen get on with their task unheeded.

But this may simply have been that Chatwin did not see the point of such adaptations. Writing to Charles Way in the summer of 1985 he had mentioned that film options had been bought on the book: "But I'm afraid I can't take too much interest in it because, on the whole, I loathe films — and particularly films doctored for a so-called television audience." While the filming was going on in the Black Mountains, Chatwin's new book was going through the press. The *Times Literary Supplement* reviewer had asked, in her piece on *On The Black Hill*: "Where on earth, one wonders, will Bruce Chatwin go next?" His readers were about to find out.

5. THE WHITE NOMAD

There was to be a five year gap between the publication in 1982 of *On The Black Hill* and *The Songlines* in 1987. The space was filled with travel and research — in early 1984, for example, Chatwin left the Adelaide Festival, where he had been appearing with contemporary British writers like Salman Rushdie and Angela Carter, to explore the central Australian desert. Those critics who thought that *On The Black Hill* represented a return by Chatwin to British themes and locations were being proved wrong. *The Songlines* turned out to be Chatwin's most financially successful work and in some sense it is the culmination of his lifelong obsession with the theme he defined in the book as being for him "the question of questions: the nature of human restlessness". The great unwritten book, 'The Nomadic Alternative', deposited its residue here in the carefully arranged selections from the notebooks that had been filled, across a life of wandering, with observations, quotations, ambitious speculations and dizzying hypotheses. The book represents a climax in Chatwin's intellectual life — he had now got some of these theoretical obesssions off his chest — and the new direction represented by the novella *Utz* which quickly followed it a year later was towards a new lightness of touch whose fruits we were denied by his premature death. A new route was opening up in his writing which we were not destined to travel down with him. Chatwin was haunted in his writing of *The Songlines* by his own illness and, knowing more about it, his readers, too, can register some of the terminal urgency in it, the desire to get some of this material down before it was too late. This was certainly his friend Salman Rushdie's conviction:

I come to think of Bruce's unwritten book as the burden he's been carrying all his writing life. Once he's done this, I think, he'll be free, he'll be able to take flight in all sorts of directions.

The thing I find saddest about *Utz* is that it suggests to me that Bruce was indeed beginning that new, light-spirited phase of flight. *Utz* is all we have of what had become possible for him once his Australian odyssey helped him express the ideas which he'd carried about for so many years. (Rushdie, 1991, p.235)

By the early 1980s Chatwin was a successful and established author and throughout the decade was much in demand as a writer of introductions to travel writing classics like Robert Byron's *The Road to Oxiana*, Osip Mandelstam's *Journey to Armenia*, and Sybille Bedford's *A Visit to Don Otavio*. Sometimes, however, the results of these occasional commissions were less than happy. In 1983 he was asked to write the introduction to a book of photographs by the controversial photographer Robert Mapplethorpe entitled *Lady Lisa Lyon*. Lisa Lyon was a Californian who had attracted considerable publicity when she won the first women's world bodybuilding championship in Los Angeles in 1979. She was the only female member of Gold's Gym in LA. Chatwin begins zestfully with a characteristic cameo of Mapplethorpe: "a New York photographer with an amused grin and coaxing amber eyes who, about ten years ago, made a name for himself with his haunting portraits of women and series of 'sex pictures' that froze — in more or less liturgical poses — the intimate activities of the so-called leather scene." The photographer was "fascinated by the satanic" and "confronts his night-biased world with the elegant and melancholic stance of the dandy". Reviewing these pictures of the (mostly unclothed) Lady Lisa, Chatwin admits candidly that "some of his pictures verge towards kitsch", a verdict that is easy to assent to. Undeterred, Chatwin races on to define Mapplethorpe as the visual equivalent of the novelist:

The photographer and his model have conspired to tell a story of their overlapping obsessions. Their glorification of the body is an act of will, a defiance of nihilism and abstraction, a story of the Modern Movement in reverse. Obscurely, in images brassy and bizarre, they are signalling a message. Perhaps the owner of this book will read into its pages an allegory for the final years of this winded century? (Chatwin, 1983)

Or alternatively the reader might see it as an assemblage of kitsch and modish Manhattan narcissism lent literary 'class' by the distinguished author of its introduction. Part of the exhilaration of Chatwin's writing is its willingness to take intellectual risks, to go to the edge of a precipice that more cautious or prosaic writers would back away from. If this is a rare moment where he tumbles over into windy nonsense it is also a reminder of how often he got it exactly right, achieving a perfect equipoise between common sense and intellectual passion.

Salman Rushdie, in an essay 'Travelling with Chatwin' written in 1989 and published in his collection *Imaginary Homelands*, set down some of his memories of his travels with Chatwin in early 1984. As they drove around the central Australian desert in a Toyota Land Cruiser, they talked endlessly about the emerging subject of Chatwin's next book. Rushdie shared his friend's fascination with the theme ("How could writers fail to love a world which has been mapped by stories?") and found himself envying him his subject. It is clear that Chatwin did most of the talking: "I am a fairly garrulous person myself," admitted Rushdie, "but in Bruce's company I don't manage more than a few interruptions. I start becoming rather proud of these." His companion "talks about everything under the sun" and the talk is peppered with the erudite and the outlandish. Sometimes Chatwin pulled out one of his famous moleskin notebooks in which "he seemed to have the phone numbers of everyone on the planet" and, in a country full of Bruces simply dialled and announced: "Bruce here." There was no need to explain who it was, for "No other Bruce ever sounded quite like Bruce."

At this stage, Chatwin was planning to call his book *Arkady* after the character in it who he later maintained was modelled on Rushdie. The latter denies the paternity and said there was a far more obvious model in Alice Springs. The book was to have been a Platonic dialogue in which two men sit under a tree in Alice "letting their talk range across time and space". Rushdie felt that Chatwin was "using me to help him have a rough draft of this talk".

In the end the formal model for *The Songlines* was the eighteenth century French dialogue novel, exemplified by Denis Diderot's *Jacques Le Fataliste*. Chatwin was attracted to the form because it had enabled the *philosophes* of the eighteenth century to realise a way of "expressing serious concepts very lightly indeed". The book had a great deal of weight to bear and he knew that he would have to give much thought to the way in which that deep substance was to be conveyed. Like all his books it presented a problem of definition. Was it a travel book or was it a novel? He insisted that it was fiction and had a running battle with his publishers as to whether it was to be classified as such or as non-fiction. He pointed with satisfaction to the Spanish term *novela de viaje* applicable to *Don Quixote*. Undoubtedly, it had fictional elements, but it was also based often on real people and real events and one of those real people was Bruce Chatwin. Other real people objected violently to the way they were portrayed in the book and one, the Australian art dealer Daphne Williams who saw herself as the abrasive dealer in Chapter 34 who tries to underpay her Aboriginal suppliers, considered taking legal action when the book appeared. Her colleague Rebecca Hossack, owner of a London gallery specialising in Aboriginal art, said that Chatwin had been writing about the Papunya-Tula co-operative of artists and that Chatwin "went along uninvited and didn't even say hello, but just stood there with a notebook". Salman Rushdie feared that the radicals of Alice Springs, people working as lawyers for the Land Rights movement, for example, would also not like what he wrote: "He said he knew, but what could one do? You had to tell it as you saw it." This approach, and these reactions, have the specificity of fault-finding normally associated with a non-fictional work. Chatwin himself told Michael Ignatieff in an interview that he didn't think there was a division between fiction and non-fiction: "There definitely should be but I don't know where it is. I've always written very close to the line." He had once tried the experiment of "counting up the lies" in *In Patagonia*, and it hadn't been "too bad" but when he came to tot up the inventions in *The Songlines* "there would be no question in my mind that the whole thing added up to a fictional work". When it came down to it, he believed: "To write it as a fiction gives you a greater flexibility; otherwise, if you were laying down the law on these subjects, and indeed I had a go at laying down the law, I can't tell you how pretentious you sound." He conceded that the imaginary dialogue "in which both narrator and interlocutor

had the liberty to be wrong" was a "difficult concept for Eng-
lish-speaking readers" but he saw no other way. Perhaps the
most satisfactory way of assigning it a generic label is to say
that it was a fictionalised narrative or inquiry. The novel is a
traditionally elastic concept but it would be stretching its roomy
walls too far to claim *The Songlines* for the genre.

The book was written in peculiar circumstances. It was completed in the summer of 1986 under what its author described
as "difficult conditions". He said that he had picked up "a very
rare fungus of the bone-marrow" in China (an ingenious and
actually erroneous diagnosis that was to receive many more
elaborations). He was certain that he was going to die: "I decided to finish the text and put myself into the hands of doctors.
My work would then be done." In a piece composed when he
was indeed in his last months of life he wrote:

> The last third of the manuscript was a commonplace book of
> quotations and vignettes intended to back up the main line of
> argument. I put this into shape on sweltering summer days,
> wrapped in shawls, shivering with cold in front of the kitchen stove.
> It was a race for time. (Chatwin, 1989, p.63)

In the event, he made what looked like a miraculous recovery
and the book came out in June 1987. It did very well (although
"the academics were cautious") but when it appeared on top of
the best seller lists Chatwin had "a crisis of confidence". He
asked himself: "Had I at last joined the trash artists?" It is clear
that he had not, and the book's popularity demonstrates that
the reading public is more adventurous than it is sometimes
given credit for. There was also Chatwin's by now formidable
reputation as writer of great talent and originality, and there
was a greater receptivity to the sort of argument that he was
putting forward. This ranged from a new awareness of the political rights of Australia's aboriginal inhabitants through to a
new 'green' awareness of the importance of the relationship of
human beings to the earth. Chatwin's large, confident generali-
sations about such matters, his essentially benign and pacific
view of human nature in relation to its environment, would
strike a chord with a generation increasingly interested in — if
not necessarily wholly endorsing — that loose collection of phil-
osophies and attitudes sometimes labelled New Age. What,

then, is *The Songlines* about?

The most concise summing-up of the book's argument was provided by Chatwin in the *Granta* interview where he tells Michael Ignatieff:

> The songlines are a labyrinth of invisible pathways which stretch to every corner of Australia. Aboriginal creation myths tell of the legendary totemic ancestors —part animal, part man— who create themselves and then set out on immense journeys across the continent, singing the name of everything that crosses their path and so singing the world into existence. In fact, there's hardly a rock or a creek or a stand of eucalyptus that isn't an 'event' on one or other of the songlines. In other words, the whole of Australia can be read as a musical score... (*Granta*, p.31)

We are not told what drew Chatwin to Australia or how he first discovered the concept of the songlines (though his extensive reading in the literature of the nomadic peoples must have drawn it to his attention) but its seductive mix of poetry and apparent anthropological fact, its endorsement of his reading of the fundamental laws of human nature, the hypothesis that *homo sapiens* was a migratory species that needed to go on journeys "whose function was to make friendly contact with neighbours near and far" and that "Man is a talking creature, a singing creature", naturally good in Rousseau's sense, proved irresistible.

> I felt the songlines were the most fascinating concept I'd ever had to deal with. I still don't quite know what implications to draw from them. But I do know they make nonsense of the various theories touted around in the name of science: that man is a territorial predator whose impulse is to raid or destroy his neighbour. (*Ibid,*)

Chatwin realised, too, that there was a personal element in all this. He accepted his interviewer's suggestion that the book could also be read as "a pretty grandiose metaphysics of your own restlessness". And he probably realised that, if nothing else, this was going to be his biggest book. He wrote to Charles Way from "a suite of cool blue rooms in a Rajput Fort" in India in March 1985: "I had no idea, when I set out to do the current book, what an enormous enterprise I'd let myself in for. I, who liked to think of myself as a kind of miniaturist, am now faced with hundreds and hundreds of chaotic pages. But I think that's the way it has to be. Every book — though of course not a play — seems to have its length predicated by the opening paragraphs, and one simply has to go on to the bitter end and take stock of the matter." Chatwin did not merely write about movement: he wrote on the move. The manuscript, like that of *On The Black Hill*, took shape in various places (parts of it, for example, were written at the Greek home of the travel writer Patrick Leigh Fermor).

Chatwin was wise to give so much thought to how he was to deal with this large subject, so much of which was right at the speculative edge, located in an intellectual no-man's-land beyond science, anthropology, or any traditional method of conducting an ethnographic inquiry. To prevent it collapsing he devised a narrative framework in which nothing much happens in the sense of plot development, but which keeps the reader's interest, keeps up the pace, and keeps up a vivid picturing of the Australian landscape and its human occupants.

The book opens with a vivid evocation of Alice Springs which demonstrates Chatwin's own ability to "sing into being" the observed world ("a grid of scorching streets where men in long white socks were forever getting in and out of Land Cruisers"). The narrator, 'Bruce', encounters in Alice a 33-year-old Russian-Australian, Arkady Volchok, who is to become the other half of the philosophical dialogue, like Jacques to his Master in *Jacques Le Fataliste* (although there is nothing in the Arkady/Bruce relationship equivalent to the wily antagonism and witty subversion of Jacques towards his master that itself helps to construct the philosophical meaning of Diderot's book; Bruce and Arkady tend to agree with each other). Innate restlessness sends him away from his Adelaide suburb, away from "the hugger-mugger of Anglo-Saxon suburbia", to work for the engineers building a new Alice Springs-Darwin railway. This involves him mapping the sacred sites of the Aboriginals by driving the traditional landowners over their old hunting grounds to identify a safe path for the permanent way. Arkady identifies with these "old men" and is, like Bruce, "astonished by their intellectual vigour, their feats of memory and their capacity and will to survive". Like them, he has few possessions and is "a tireless bushwalker". He is also struck by the beauty of the concept of the songlines which receives its first attempt at definition in the opening pages. Once again, he sounds like Chatwin, who also seized ideas with an aesthetic as much as an intellectual passion. Although Arkady recognises that the hunting and gathering days of the Aboriginals are over: "What could be done for Aboriginals was to preserve their most essential liberty: the liberty to remain poor." They seem wiser and more thoughtful than ever "in a Europe of mindless materialism".

If Arkady is often a fairly transparent mouthpiece for the thoughts of the real Bruce he also fulfils another important function. Unlike an "envious academic" anthropologist from Canberra who betrayed some Aboriginal lore, Arkady has so won the confidence of the elders of the Walbiri tribe that they invite him to witness their secret ceremonies and encourage him to learn their songs. He is therefore Bruce's guide into the mysteries of the songlines and to the people who follow their invisible tracery. Arkady steers Bruce past the self-regarding urban radicals who have taken up the Land Rights issue, past the truculent backwoodsmen, and the instinctively suspicious guardians of secret knowledge, into the charmed circle where Bruce always wished to be. Only the right people, Chatwin seems to be saying, should be entrusted with certain inquiries. Arkady is two steps ahead of Bruce but treats him with an amiable indulgence. He is one of them. In fact, Chatwin must have encountered much hostility as well as genuine difficulties put in his way by the gap in language and understanding between him and the subjects of his inquiry. Colin Thubron worried about the validity of Chatwin's quest and told an interviewer in 1991: "I admire what Bruce did in *The Songlines*. It is a remarkable piece of writing. But in the end I just don't believe his thesis. What I am admitting is that we cannot fully make sense of another culture. We cannot overcome that difference." Other friends of Chatwin had the same anxiety about his project and Michael Ignatieff said he was struck by "the edginess, the bitterness of your relationship with these Aboriginal pre-Socratics". He wanted to know how much closer Chatwin could have got to them:

> I would have chosen to go and live on an Aboriginal settlement.
> Then I would have had to undergo some kind of ritual initiation.
> But my stance was to remain an observer, to get as close as I possibly

could without going through all that. I just didn't want to. (*Granta,* p.34)

Chatwin was conceding the limitations of his involvement and admitting he had been forced on to "tricky ground". But he insisted: "If I had become involved, I wouldn't write the books I do." Salman Rushdie, a more political animal than either Ignatieff or Chatwin, was concerned that when he and Chatwin together met the "young white radicals" in Alice Springs they distrusted him "for his apparent political conservatism and his 'anthropological' orientation" but that his friend was untroubled: "walking blithely through the minefield of black Australian politics with unconcern". John Bayley, reviewing the book in *The London Review of Books,* expressed the concern that the transmission of concepts like the songlines or the "dreaming tracks" from an Aboriginal language into English might somehow "take away their meaning by making them sound interesting and mysterious. But poetry is what gets lost in translation." Chatwin is dealing with the concept, analysing it, naming it, in another language with a different conceptual hinterland. We are always at some distance from the life of the idea in the mind of the Aboriginal. Moreover he is relating it to the concerns of a European writer ("the Europe of mindless materialism", for instance) which may have no point of intersection with those of its originating culture. But how could it be otherwise? The traveller's tale is always a report back to the rest of us, shaped in our terms, with the emphases determined by the presuppositions of the receiving culture. All we can say is that Chatwin was fully aware of the dilemma (though he did not discuss the issue of language or translation) and was prepared to take a risk in order that something might be discovered.

As with *In Patagonia,* the book, very early on, establishes a personal grounding for the idea of the quest. Chatwin associates a childhood picture in his great aunt's library of an Aboriginal family on the move with the "fantastic homelessness" of his first five years and recalls an image from the same period of the Aboriginals "who one day would be working happily on a cattle-station: the next, without a word of warning and *for no good reason,* would up sticks and vanish into the blue".

But soon the dialogue is well into its stride. Arkady, although dazzingly gifted, sometimes sounds "like a man on a public platform" which is Chatwin's way of sounding a note of sceptical alertness. The quick and vivid pace of the narrative offsets an incipient tendency towards stiltedness in some of these exchanges, where Bruce is seldom seen to lose the advantage in repartee. Arkady, for instance, is holding forth, over a Todd Street cappuccino, on the need for the land to be left untouched as it was in the Dreamtime when the Ancestors sang the world into existence:

> 'Rilke', I said, 'had a similar intuition. He also said song was existence.'
> 'I know,' said Arkady, resting his chin on his hands. '"Third Sonnet to Orpheus".' (*The Songlines*, p.13)

The reader is, or is meant to be, impressed by the erudite pair. Bruce adopts a sceptical stance during these coffee-house Socratics but of course Arkady is voicing pure Chatwinism: "The Aboriginals, he went on, were a people who trod lightly over the earth; and the less they took from the earth, the less they had to give in return...The wars of the twentieth century are the price for having taken too much." Bruce is also aware of the limitations of the quest he has embarked on:

> My reason for coming to Australia was to try to learn for myself and not from other men's books, what a Songline was — and how it worked. Obviously, I was not going to get to the heart of the matter, nor would I want to. (*The Songlines*, p.14)

But the dialogue is light and springy enough to sustain an already evolving account of the nature of the songlines without giving way and without the reader losing interest either in the intellectual content or the more concrete narrative of Bruce and Arkady's journey out of Alice. Chatwin's memorable and sharp phrase-making also helps: "the whole of Australia can be read as a musical score...a spaghetti of Iliads and Odysseys, writhing this way and that...recreated the Creation". When Arkady begins to interrogate Bruce about his reasons for coming to Australia we are obviously hearing Chatwin interrogating himself. And it is fascinating to eavesdrop. He tells Arkady the story of what is the real Bruce's life: the rejection of Sotheby's and the recuperative trip to the Sudan where:

> . . .at night, lying awake under the stars, the cities of the West seemed sad and alien — and the pretensions of the 'art world' idiotic. Yet here I had a sense of homecoming... I felt I had to know the secret of their [the nomads'] timeless and irreverent vitality... The more I read, the more convinced I became that nomads had been the crankhandle of history... (*The Songlines*, pp.20-21)

In Alice, Bruce discovers the Aboriginal artists, shyly coming into the galleries where their art is skilfully marketed, Government subsidy having created "an instant, Australian school of abstract painting". An American tourist buys a picture of a honey-ant dreaming, after the artist explains it to her and she knows "that the painting was a thing done for white men, but he had given her a glimpse of something rare and strange, and she was very grateful" — another hint of Chatwin's sense of the limitations — and the gains — of his quest. In Alice, too, Bruce meets an altogether unattractive group of pro-Aboriginal activists, whose unappealing self-righteousness and dogmatism, may be a strategy to pre-empt criticisms of the kind they are actually voicing. There is an edgy irony in the account of a slightly less rebarbative group of the concerned at a barbecue: "All of them, I guess, worked in one way or other with or for the Aboriginals. They were young and had wonderful legs." An engaging barrister tells Bruce with an irony we can savour: "Arkady tells me you've got all sorts of interesting theories about this and that." It is clear from these passages — and the accounts of Rushdie also confirm it — that Chatwin met activists like these during his Australian researches and there must have been many uncomfortable moments, given the highly charged nature of the Land Rights issue in contemporary Australia. Later he meets Father Flynn, the first Aboriginal to take charge of his own mission and another expert on the lore of his own people. Bruce gradually breaks down the resistance of Flynn, plagued as he is by "nutters" with theories about the songlines. But why is Bruce any different from them?

Flynn is able to take the definitions forward again. He explains that Aboriginals had the idea that all goods were malign and would work against their possessors "unless they were forever in motion". The songlines, however, were a form of trade route with "songs, not things, the principal medium of exchange". A particular song-cycle "went leapfrogging through language barriers...a Dreaming Track might...thread its way through twenty languages or more; and go on to hit the sea near Adelaide". Flynn's exegesis is not addressed to the sceptical intelligence: he proposes that, in the Dreamtime, a pregnant woman would step on a couplet and the "spirit-child" would work its way through an open callus on her foot, say, and up into her womb where it would "impregnate the foetus with song". The child when born would find a "conception site" had been reserved for him or her and the elders would have decided "which stanzas will be the child's private property". These elaborations, which often strain credulity, have an undeniable imaginative appeal, and besides, we are not given any insight into where these explanations come from. They are always mediated through semi-outsiders who have become initiate and have obviously been developed in oral tradition; there are no documentary sources to cite. Since there is no possibility of critical challenge it is far easier just to succumb to the poetic beauty of the conceptual scheme being described.

Bruce reads Strehlow's *Songs of Central Australia* and discovers a kindred spirit who: "Having grasped the connection of song and land...wished to strike at the roots of song itself: to find in song a key to unravelling the mysteries of the human condition. It was an impossible undertaking." The fact of an undertaking being impossible was no barrier to Bruce Chatwin. Stimulated by Strehlow's "great and lonely book", Bruce goes back to his Alice motel, pulls out his yellow pad and starts to write a brief imaginative account of the Aboriginal creation myth, "In the Beginning". It shows how much *The Songlines* depends on its structure of dialogue, its irony, humour, vivid description, and characters, for without any of these elements this is a rather bland and uninteresting piece. The book is kept alive by its characters: Father Terence in his hermitage by the Timor Sea writing a manual of poverty, the 73-year-old Communist Jim Hanlon whose bracing response to the author's subject matter is: "Sacred bloody baloney! What these boys need is Organization!", or the iron-pumping policeman whose favourite book is Spinoza's *Ethics*. Fanciful some of the speculations may be, but the actuality of contemporary Australia is in the book: the fitful racism, the occasional hostility to the Old Marlburian Pom, the dusty Aboriginal camps with their "humpies", the motels and truck stops, and the beautiful women like Arkady's girlfriend Marian who emerges from a shower "like a Piero madonna":

> So what was it, I wondered, about these Australian women? Why were they so strong and satisfied, and so many of the men so drained? (*The Songlines*, p.112)

Before leaving Alice, Arkady presents Bruce with a copy of Ovid's *Metamorphoses* and he frequently invokes the ancient classics for purposes of comparison, reflecting, his critics might argue, the Eurocentric bias of his inquiry. The song of the Lizard Ancestor, for example, which is performed for him in one Aboriginal settlement is the story of "an antipodean Helen". Recalling, one day in the desert, a blustery day in Greece reading Ovid in Arcadia: "it struck me, from what I now knew of the songlines, that the whole of Classical mythology might represent the relics of a giant 'song-map': that all the to-ing and fro-ing...could all be interpreted in terms of totemic geography". Chatwin's project was always to discover universal concepts which exposed underlying connections of this kind.

Chatwin represents the Aboriginals positively but not completely without a critical perspective. He describes a teacher called Lydia who fears her son's involvement with the Pintupi tribe's secrets: "she had an idea that the Aboriginals with their terrifying immobility, had somehow got Australia by the throat. There was an awesome power in these apparently passive people who would sit, watch, wait and manipulate the white man's guilt".

About half way through *The Songlines* there is a distinct shift in Chatwin's method. Arrived at Mount Cullen he meets a white man in a caravan reading Proust and turning over big ideas far from a civilisation he judges corrupt. This is Rolf Niehart, a Prussian-French intellectual and storekeeper who gives Arkady and Bruce a caravan to stay in. Arkady soon has to go on an errand to Alice by plane and at last Bruce is left alone with the opportunity to write. He has already said that his intention in coming to Australia was to find the space to shape his lifetime's perceptions about nomadism into a piece of writing. He makes three piles of the famous moleskin notebooks crammed with his research notes, quotations, ideas, speculations. Chatwin bought these notebooks — *carnets moleskines* — from a *papeterie* in the Rue de l'Ancienne Comedie in Paris and took them everywhere with him. Hearing that supplies were about to dry up he ordered a hundred from the Paris shop but was told it was too late. The manufacturer had died. In referring to the notebooks he is preparing the ground for opening them up to the reader. Up to now, the book has been a lively travel narrative interspersed with speculation about the songlines. But something else is about to happen:

> I had a presentiment that the 'travelling' phase of my life might be passing. I felt, before the malaise of settlement crept over me, that I should re-open those notebooks. I should set down on paper a resumé of the ideas, quotations and encounters which had amused and obsessed me; and which I hoped would shed light on what is for me the question of questions: the nature of human restlessness. (*The Songlines*, p.181)

The 'novel' now asks its readers to put the narrative on the shelf for a moment and consider a carefully arranged pattern of quotations and longer descriptions of Chatwin's encounters with anonymous desert wanderers and famous thinkers such as Konrad Lorenz. He admitted in an interview that "the juxtapositions are artful" and was impressed by an essay of Walter Benjamin in which he said that the ideal book would be a book of quotations. He also had the example of a commonplace book by the Viennese poet and essayist Hugo Von Hofmannsthal which was "a sort of dialogue of quotations and his own thoughts as well, all jammed in". The section of the book that begins at page 183 with 'From the Notebooks' takes its bearings from Pascal's thought that "all our miseries stemmed from a single cause: our inability to remain quietly in a room":

> Our nature lies in movement; complete calm is death. (from Pascal, *Pensées, The Songlines*, p.183)

Chatwin speculated whether "our need for distraction, our mania for the new, was, in essence, an instinctive migratory urge akin to that of birds in autumn". All the Great Teachers (Chatwin was fond of the portentous initial capital) had preached that "Man...to rediscover his humanity...must slough off his attachments and take to the road". He had long entertained the conjecture that natural selection has designed us "for a career of seasonal journeys *on foot* through a blistering land of thorn-scrub or desert". Chatwin believed that "life is a journey to be walked on foot" and long ago had told someone in Patagonia that "my God is the god of walkers". He had also talked of "the sacramental aspect of walking" and the fact that "the act of journeying contributes towards a sense of physical and mental well-being". Yet paradoxically, only one, brief, and soon-abandoned walk is described in *The Songlines* — for much of the book his peripatetic deity is the Toyota Land Cruiser. Mobility in a less elevated metaphysical sense was also crucial to Bruce Chatwin. When *The Songlines* was published he told *The Daily Mail* in a publicity interview: "When a situation gets difficult my first instinct is to flee." He practised what he preached, for his life became a restless journey and he said that he could not write unless he travelled.

The reader who has accompanied Chatwin this far will have caught his enthusiasm for the book's main line of inquiry with the result that he can count on a measure of tolerance for this new departure. But if he had simply shaken out the contents of his notebooks on to the floor, so to speak, that tolerance would quickly have evaporated. His skill was to arrange quotations that reinforced and gave sanction to his theme and to intersperse them, rich and suggestive as they all are, with accounts of the extraordinary incidents that he had witnessed in a life of travelling and to retell them with his customary skill. The core narrative of the book is not abandoned, and is frequently returned to, but it no longer holds centre stage which is taken by this new material. The quotations come from Darwin, Robert Burton, author of *The Anatomy of Melancholy* ("we should be ever in motion"), Kierkegaard ("I have walked myself into my best thoughts") and, again and again, from Rimbaud: *"l'homme aux semelles de vent"*. They are the distillations, like perfume, of a lifetime's wandering. Chatwin believed that wandering "re-establishes the original harmony which once existed between man and the universe" and that walking "dissolved crimes of violence". The nomadic peoples — often judged aberrant and barbarian by the settlers and city dwellers — were in fact, like the

Aboriginals, uninterested in conflicts over territory. "The tradition of the camp-fire faces that of the Pyramid," reads the quotation from Martin Buber and another suggests that "no people but the Jews have ever felt more keenly the moral ambiguities of settlement". The Islamic philosopher of history Ib'n Khaldun "based his system on the intuition that men decline, morally and physically, as they drift towards cities". The Tibetan word for a human being is one who goes on migrations and the Hadj is a ritual migration, "to detach men from their sinful homes and reinstate, if temporarily, the equality of all men before God".

Chatwin realised that this ideal picture of the nomads could be taken too far. There was a tradition of vendetta amongst the Arabs and nomads had often sold themselves as mercenaries: "Any nomad tribe is a military machine in embryo whose impulse, if not to fight other nomads, is to raid or threaten the city." If the Cain and Abel story represents some kind of duality in human nature, the origins of the state, Chatwin believed, were as "a kind of chemical fusion between herdsman and planter".

After forty-six pages of this epigrammatic mosaic, Bruce returns to his narrative and goes on an abortive hunting expedition with his Aboriginal friends but soon he is back to the notebook material to deal with the nature of human aggression. He rejected intellectual pessimism about human nature such as that expounded by Arthur Koestler and believed instead that men were products of their situation and that "learning conditions everything they will ever say or do". This did not, however, seem to rule out a belief in "a core of unmodifiable instinct". Chatwin feared that a world shorn of instinct "would be a far more deadly and dangerous place than anything the 'aggression-mongers' could come up with". He next moves on to the Hero Cycle which "represents an unchangeable paradigm of 'ideal' behaviour for the human male". He once made the experiment of slotting the career of Che Guevara on to the structure of the Beowulf epic and it seemed to him to fit. Myths, for Chatwin, were "coded messages of instinct". He recalled a meeting with Konrad Lorenz in Austria in 1974 where the idea of defence rather than aggression was discussed between them (the dialogue ended characteristically with Lorenz declaring:

"What you have just said is totally new"). Chatwin's new thought was that at some time in the evolutionary past the species had experienced some terrible ordeal with the Beast (he felt that the blood-vengeance and terrible initation rites of the Aboriginals "might stem from the fact of their having no proper beasts to contend with"). The howling and unease of babies left alone "could be explained by the constant presence of predators in the primeval home of man" he speculated. When Chatwin launches a hypothesis of this kind we might legitimately ask what standard of proof, what principle of verification, enables us to assess it. He seems to sidestep the more pedestrian forms of scientific method by choosing concepts of such a kind and expressed in such a language that it is difficult to contest them.

Chatwin himself quarrels with the South African scientist Raymond Dart who falsified the evidence to confirm "the predatory transition from Ape to Man" and follows instead the critique of the anthropological excavator Bob Brain, who resolved that the assertion that "murder made man" made no evolutionary sense. The argument here becomes more dense and speculative and the reader may well be tempted to riffle forward through the pages in search of more particular writing. Yet, however speculative the tone and the language it reaches to the heart of Chatwin's belief that "man was born in the desert" in the scrub of thorn whose elemental austerity he still pines for. With Bob Brain's findings he concluded ("an idea to send the head spinning") that early man was preyed upon by a specialist killer of primates, *dinofelis*, and that he actually defeated this original Prince of Darkness. The result was that the whole of history has been "a search for false monsters" or "a nostalgia for the Beast we have lost". In short — and one in the eye for the theorists of human aggression — "man, in becoming man, got the better of the powers of destruction". Tribal fighting and warfare were not a part of the original scheme of things: defence against the common predator dictated "only the classical forms of co-operation". The selections from the notebooks stop a few chapters before the end of the book. Chatwin makes his last attempt to sum up the nature of the songlines, drawing on such cognate ideas as the ley lines, the "dragon lines" about which he had written elsewhere, the Lapp "singing stones" or the Nazca lines about which he had also written. Convinced that the concept was universal, he made one last leap into the Empyrean:

> And here I must take a leap into faith: into regions I would not expect anyone to follow.
>
> I have a vision of the Songlines stretching across the continents and ages; that wherever men have trodden they have left a trail of song (of which we may, now and then, catch an echo); and that these trails must reach back, in time and space, to an isolated pocket in the African Savannah, where the First Man opening his mouth in defiance of the terrors that surrounding him, shouted the opening stanza of the World Song, 'I AM!'. (*The Songlines*, p.314)

With this final bold speculation Chatwin rests his case.

The book ends with a final chapter in which Bruce and Arkady drive an Aboriginal called Limpy to Cycad Valley, a place of immense importance on his personal songline, where the tjuringa (the sacred board that represents the wanderings of his Dreamtime ancestor) is stored and where three of his distant relatives are dying. As they approach, Limpy makes them slow down the vehicle to the walking pace appropriate to his Native Cat couplets and eventually spots the three men in a clearing lying on bare hospital bedsteads, facing death like the mystics who believe that the ideal man walks himself to a "right death". As Chatwin put it, "he who has arrived 'goes back' ":

> They knew where they were going, smiling at death in the shade of a ghost-gum. (*The Songlines*, p.327)

There was a personal imprint on these last words, as Chatwin later explained in an interview:

> I wrote that last chapter about three old men dying under a gum tree, when I was just about to conk myself. It was done with great speed. I often have to labour over sentences, but this time I just wrote it straight down on a yellow pad, and that was the end of the book. It did bring home how writing a fiction impinges on your life. (*Granta*, p.35)

Chatwin was to survive barely more than a year longer and write one more work of fiction but he must have felt on completing *The Songlines* that something had come to an end. If Rushdie was right a new phase was about to begin with *Utz*.

That brief novella was to be its only fruit.

But the Australian book was a critical and popular success. Two of the most distinguished travel writers, Patrick Leigh Fermor and Colin Thubron, chose it as their book of the year in *The Spectator* that Christmas. Thubron called it: "The most memorable book of my year, Bruce Chatwin's *The Songlines*, is distinguished by that least British of traits: intellectual passion. A melange of fiction, travel and anthropology, it develops into a unique study of nomadism — of all human restlessness". Leigh Fermor, reviewing the book earlier in the year in the same journal, had described it as "a fascinating, extraordinary and rather puzzling book". John Bayley in *The London Review of Books* was equally puzzled but concluded: "Whatever it is about, the book is a masterpiece." Edmund White, in *The Sunday Times*, wrote: "Towards the end of his life Sartre wondered why people still write novels; had he read Chatwin's he might have found new excitement in the genre." And the book went straight to the top of the *Sunday Times* bestseller list and stayed in the top ten for nine months. 'The Nomadic Alternative' had finally been exorcised and the process had been a triumph in spite of the unorthodoxy of the form and the risky nature of its speculative ambitions.

6. LOOKING EAST

"The writers I adore are nearly always the Russians," Bruce Chatwin declared. At his death he was reported to have been contemplating a 'Russian' novel. He made frequent visits to Russia and to Eastern Europe, not as the result of any ideological prompting, but because he loved the art and literature of the East. In the imaginary dialogue with the Russian Arkady Volchok, in Chapter 9 of *The Songlines*, 'Bruce' sympathises with Arkady's father who wishes to return to his homeland:

> 'Even as a Westerner,' I said, 'I know how he must feel. Whenever I've been to Russia, I can't wait to get away. Then I can't wait to go back.' (*The Songlines*, p.43)

Arkady wants to know why Bruce loves Russia. "Hard to say...I like to think of Russia as a land of miracles. Just as you fear the worst, something wonderful always happens."

Chatwin travelled to Russia many times, the first occasion being when he was employed by Sotheby's as an art expert. He also visited Russia on assignments for *The Sunday Times* and met a grumpy and disillusioned Nadezhda Mandelstam in her Moscow apartment. He pacified her with three jars of his mother's home-made marmalade and listened to her growling: "And in Russia we have no grand writers left." Chatwin adored her husband Osip Mandelstam's *Journey to Armenia* which he took with him on his travels. In 1989 he wrote an introduction to the Redstone Press edition of Clarence Brown's translation of this "breathtaking, elliptical prose" which first appeared in the Soviet magazine *Zvezda* in 1933. Its publication, he wrote, was a miracle "but then Russia was (as it still is) a land of miracles". Chatwin also admired Mandelstam's "miraculous" essay 'Conversation with Dante' which contained the thought that the *Divine Comedy* glorified "the human gait, the measure and rhythm of walking, the foot and its shape". Mandelstam, in an *aperçu* that went straight into the moleskin notebook, continued: "The step, linked to the breathing and saturated with thought: this Dante understands as the beginning of prosody."

In January 1973, "on a morning of Stygian gloom", Chatwin called on Konstantin Melnikov, the architect, at his house on Krivoarbatsky Lane in Moscow. The visit came at the end of a two week spell in Moscow "trying to ferret out survivors from the heady days of the leftist art movement of the early twenties" during which he had supper with the daughter of the artist Rodchenko and sat on Mayakovsky's bentwood chair. Melnikov's house was "one of the architectural wonders of the twentieth century" although now rather dilapidated, and its creator was plainly a frustrated visionary. He spent forty years in the house, isolated by the authorities, and in his lonely seclusion and dedication to art he calls to mind Kaspar Joachim Utz. In February Chatwin visited George Kostakis, the leading private art collector in the Soviet Union who had rescued the products of the Futurist school and turned his home into a museum. Paradoxically, the authorities allowed him to keep his collection which he wished eventually to leave to a State museum. Again, the parallels with Utz seem unignorable.

In the autumn of 1982, Chatwin had spent ten September days "sailing smoothly down the Volga" on the MV Maxim Gorky. Chatwin was reading Gorky, Tolstoy and Pushkin and recalled that Chekhov took a Volga cruise for his honeymoon in 1901. The French-speaking Intourist guide was excited by Chatwin's friendship with David Garnett, son of Edward and Constance Garnett who had met Lenin in London for the Second International. "*C'est une relique precieuse*" said the guide when he heard of Lenin's bus ticket from Tottenham Court Road to the Garnett's house in Putney which David Garnett used to keep in his wallet. At Stalingrad Chatwin thought the statue of The Motherland at Mamayev Kurgan, a hill where the Tartar Khan Mamay once pitched his royal yurt, "represented Asia, warning the West never to try and cross the Volga, never to set foot in the heartland". It was the meeting of West and East which plainly fascinated him.

In 1967, on a trip to Czechoslovakia on behalf of Sotheby's, Chatwin met a collector of Meissen porcelain who had "shrunk his horizons down to those of his best friends, who were all porcelain figures seven inches high". The man lived like a monk and Chatwin observed that it was "a fantasy of people like myself to want to sit in a cell and never move again. That's what this man did." Just as *On The Black Hill* was the anchored, immobile, alternative to the wanderings in Patagonia, the wide-open spaces of Australia in *The Songlines* ceded to the cramped, monastic cell of the collector Utz. Chatwin's books oscillated between, as it were, restlessness indulged and restlessness contained. The theme itself was never absent.

The publication of the short novel *Utz* in 1988 presented Chatwin's readers, therefore, with the usual surprise, coming as it did very quickly on the heels of the bulk and the reach of *The Songlines*. Some reviewers, however, were beginning to discern some sort of cyclical pattern at work. John Lanchester in *The London Review of Books* suggested that: "The reader who is starting to get wise to Chatwin, and particularly to the way each book of his seems to set out to contradict the expectations aroused by its immediate precursor, could construct an idea of Chatwin's new novel by reversing the postulates of his last one, *The Songlines*... Extrapolating negatively, then, we can guess that Chatwin's new novel is unsprawling, unmetaphysical, un- 18th century in tone and in technique, set in the Old World and with a central theme which has something to do with not being a nomad. And so it proves."

The first thing that strikes the reader of *Utz* is its brevity. Chatwin said that he thought of himself as a miniaturist and there is a concentrated economy in this book that is certainly not on the grand scale. But its thematic freight — the meaning, purpose, consolation, and even ultimate disappointment of art — is as substantial as any serious writer could wish for. It is short and brilliantly economical in its means but it is anything but lightweight. Chatwin once quoted admiringly Clarence Brown's account of Osip Mandelstam's prose and "the ineffable satisfaction that comes when sentences wave like flags and strut like peacocks". Chatwin's prose was virtuoso in this fashion and it was his skill as a writer was to convey *multum in parvo*. "Each sentence is fashioned, polished, and put into place with microscopic care," wrote Nicholas Shakespeare in *The Daily Telegraph*. Short as this novel is, a case could be made for its being his most perfect work.

In spite of the obvious differences of scale from its precursor, there are some pertinent similarities. Once again it is a fiction whose launching pad is fact. A real 'model' for Utz existed and the facts of the narrator's life fit with what we know of Chatwin's. His interests could plausibly be those of the writer. The big subject of nomadism may have been formally superseded but the underlying themes of restlessness and immobility, of artistic obsession, of the condition of exile, are not new ones in Chatwin's writing. And at a formal level, the opening of the book in the present with a gradual easing backwards to the beginning of the story repeats the structural method of *The Viceroy of Ouidah*. It is written, too, in the characteristic short — but for the first time unnumbered — sections which are the typical construction method of Chatwin's fictions.

As befits the story of a fanatical and meticulous collector of Meissen porcelain, the account of the funeral Utz planned for himself and with which the book opens is fastidiously rendered with an aesthete's eye. Utz's well-laid plans are partly confounded by "the wreath of Bolshevik vulgarity" that has been placed on top of the coffin. The scene is made vivid and particular by the sharpness of the observation ("In a garden across the street, jackdaws with twigs in their beaks were wheeling above the lindens, and now and then a minor avalanche would slide from the pantiled roof of a tenement") and the telling details. Dr Orlik's clutching "seven of the ten pink carnations he had hoped to afford at the florist's" writes in a few words an entire story of poverty and constraint in the same way that the two words "to whom?" (of the museum director's card of condolence) suggest the paucity of Utz's human contacts. The narrator notes of Utz's servant, Marta: "To relieve the pressure on her bunions the sides of her shoes were split open". These sharp, vivid details are effective because they are so particular, grounding the narrative in a firm sense of the actual, all the more effective because of the faintly unreal nature of life in this totalitarian state which the citizens are compelled to treat with a certain frigid humour. The two sole mourners, Orlik and Marta, toast Utz's memory at the Hotel Bristol by raising their glasses to the stuffed bear "placed there by some humorous person to remind the clientele of their country's fraternal protector". Utz was actually expecting a larger number of mourners, not least his "venal cousins" turning up "in case there was anything to be had". As usual in Chatwin's writing, human greed is routinely invoked in the presence of the art world and connoisseurship.

The narrator explains that his 1967 visit to Prague (Chatwin originally referred to the projected novella as "a memoir") was for a week of historical research on an article commissioned by a magazine editor on the Emperor Rudolf II's passion for collecting exotica. "I intended the article to be part of a larger work on the psychology — or psychopathology — of the compulsive collector." It seems a perfectly Chatwinian project. As it turned out, the narrator, owing to "idleness and my ignorance of the languages", abandons the task in favour of a holiday. He stops nonetheless at an Austrian schloss on the way to see the legendary Kunstkammer or cabinet of curiosities of Rudolf's uncle, Archduke Ferdinand, which includes "a late Roman agate tazza that might or might not be the Holy Grail". Could this detail belong anywhere else than in a sentence by Bruce Chatwin? Another of the fabulous items from the Kunstkammer that have vanished is "the phial of dust from which God created Adam". What fascinates the narrator is the obsession that would lead Rudolf to neglect his Empire and the affairs of state in order to shut himself away with his astronomers or search with his alchemists for the philosopher's stone. He is a man obsessed by curious knowledge rather than the "real world" of his Empire. Like Utz (or the two Radnorshire twins blithely ignoring the Second World War) he has slipped the moorings that should attach him to History, in the all-embracing pursuit of an idea or an obsession.

He then starts to connect this ability to absent oneself from the quotidian with the fact that Prague is an unreal city, "the most mysterious of European cities, where the supernatural was always a possibility". He believes that the Czech's "metaphysical view of life" encouraged them to "look on acts of force as ephemera". The friend of the narrator who is the source of this speculation places the "interminable whine" of the dissident artist against "the true heroes of this impossible situation" who wouldn't raise a murmur against Party or State "yet who seemed to carry the sum of Western Civilisation in their heads". This reads like an oblique reference to Mandelstam who composed poems in his head to outwit the censors. Chatwin seems to be advocating a sort of intellectual survivalism, a wise passivity preferred to an oppositional activism of the kind that was to liberate the Czechs less than two years after the book was published. He is saying that the silent dissenters "inflict a final insult on the state, by pretending it does not exist" and that the state, by trying to eliminate individualism, had in fact "offered limitless time for the intelligent individual to dream his private and heretical thoughts". He talks warmly of "a streetsweeper who had written a philosophical commentary on the Anaximander Fragment". But we might want to ask whether that streetsweeper's choice of this way of writing philosophy was in fact a choice at all. It is one thing for a thinker to choose poverty and asceticism, as Chatwin was increasingly to urge modern men and women to do, and quite another to have it forced on one. Like the Western intellectuals who took a vicarious pleasure in the dispatch of academics to the fields during China's cultural revolution, Chatwin is running the risk of a surrogate heroism that might not be valued in the same way by those who have no choice but to embrace it. One thing, however, is clear: barely a dozen expansively typeset pages into this apparently slight novella we are already in the thick of what its reviewer in *The Times*, Philip Howard, called "dirty great issues of life and death". The narrator's friend, who has been expounding these ideas, now refers him on to Utz: "a Rudolf of our time".

Utz, descended from a family of minor Saxon landowners, is the owner of a spectacular 1000-piece collection of Meissen porcelain which he has skilfully preserved throughout the War and the Stalinist years in his two-room flat on Siroka Street in Prague. The passion for collecting is first evident on a summer visit to his grandmother's house where he finds himself "bewitched" by a Meissen figurine of Harlequin. "I want him," says Kaspar simply. He had found his vocation and would "elevate his life to collecting — 'rescuing' as he came to call it— the porcelains of the Meissen factory". Like Bruce Chatwin, Utz is an obsessive collector: the former of ideas and stories, the latter of porcelains. The word 'rescue' is just, because, for Chatwin, it is typically a question of recovering and recuperating old ideas rather than embracing newly-minted ones. But if Utz is an obsessive collector, like his creator, like him also he sees the museum as a mausoleum:

> An object in a museum case...must suffer the de-natured existence of an animal in the zoo...private ownership confers on the owner the right and the need to touch. As a young child will reach out to handle the thing it names, so the passionate collector, his eye in harmony with his hand, restores to the object the life-giving touch of its maker. The collector's enemy is the museum curator. (*Utz*, p.20)

Already the theme of art as a life force, a surrogate act of creation ("the life-giving touch of its maker") has been introduced. Politically Utz was neutral and made whatever accommodations he could with the state in the higher interests of his obsession. He has the same selfish abstraction from the demands of the time as Benjamin and Lewis Jones: "Wars, pogroms and revolutions, he used to say, offer excellent opportunities for the collector." Kristallnacht was a particularly happy occasion from his point of view. History is examined through the narrow viewfinder of the obsessive. An incipient love for England where he once stayed in "a house of cats and cuckoo clocks" is abruptly terminated when a voice on the wartime BBC announces: "There is no china in Dresden today." Yet he had also collaborated with the activities of Goering's art squad by giving information as to the whereabouts of certain works of art. In doing so, he was able to protect or hide a number of his Jewish friends: "What, after all, was the value of a Titian or a Tiepolo if one human life could be saved?" The question is the narrator's; we are not entirely certain it would be posed with such clarity of conviction by Utz himself, in spite of his noble actions. The moral ambivalence of art; the indifference of beauty to history; the neglect of civic duty or natural humanity by those obsessed with the art object, are the themes woven into this account of Utz's obsession. After the war his friend Orlik suggests they flee to the West but Utz gestures to his shelves, six deep with Meissen figurines: "I cannot leave them." Possessions are inimical to movement: the wanderer must travel light.

The Communist rulers adopt a pragmatic approach to Utz and his collection. They cannot quite determine the political correctness or otherwise of the collector and realise in the end that to confiscate it would be an administrative nightmare. Orlik, too, has troubles with the Thought Police. In the delightfully humorous scene at the Restaurant Pstruh he gives an account of his research topic — the life of the *musca domestica* in the Prague Metropolitan area — and regrets that his fellow entomologists, especially the Party members, preferred those insects which exhibited more laudably correct social tendencies. To Orlik the house-fly was an anarchist and an individualist. With a fixity of habit worthy of the Jones brothers, Utz and Orlik have eaten at the Pstruh every Thursday since 1946.

When Utz and the narrator wander about the city of Prague their dialogue turns effortlessly into an intellectual debate about such things as giants and dwarfs, the latter exciting Utz because of their analogy with figurines. But there is a more intriguing topic which they broach while sitting in the Old Jewish Cemetery: the Golem. The Rabbi Loew, in Rudolf's time, was credited after his death with supernatural powers — of which fashioning the Golem Yossel "from the glutinous mud of the River Vltava" was one. Utz claims that not only was Adam the first human being created by Yahweh from "an inert mass of clay", he was also "the first ceramic sculpture". The story of Christ fashioning model birds from clay and then breathing them into fluttering life completes the identification of the porcelain-artist with the creator. Both make life out of clay. Asked if his figurines are alive, Utz will say only: "They are alive and they are dead." He is then asked if art-collecting, like golem-making, is idolatry and he agrees that it is. The narrator presses him further: do porcelains "demand their own death"? Utz replies with an enigmatic caution: "I do not know. It is a very problematic question." Certainly, there is a mortuary aspect to collecting and when the narrator finally visits Utz's flat to see the collection:

> The smell was familiar to me: the stale smell of rooms where works of art are kept, and dusting considered dangerous. (*Utz*, p.47)

The description of the flat conveys the strong sense that an alternative reality has taken over for the obsessive collector. The room is narrowed by a double bank of plate glass shelves: "The shelves were backed with mirror, so that you had the illusion of entering an enfilade of glittering chambers, a 'dream palace' multiplied to infinity, through which human forms flitted like insubstantial shadows." Collecting is partly a sickness and the ruler Augustus the Strong suffered from this *porzellankrankheit* so badly that it "so warped his vision, and that of his ministers, that their delirious schemes for ceramics got confused with real political power". The narrator, who does not entirely share Utz's obsessive regard for porcelain, makes what he thinks are the right noises but is at heart uneasy at this obsession with the half-real and forces a nervous laugh when invited to admire the comic figurines. Each figurine is marked to show that it will eventually be left to the State museum: " 'But those persons,' Utz whispered, 'have made a mistake' ". The fate of the collection is the final enigma of the book and the reader is being prepared for it.

In the 1950s, hurt by those intrusive and insensitive museum officials, Utz contemplates escape and arranges a visit to Vichy ostensibly on health grounds. He is repulsed by the vulgarity and materialism of the non-Communist world and comes to the conclusion that he is "another middle-aged, Middle-European refugee adrift in an unfriendly world" and worse than this "the most useless of refugees, an aesthete". It is only his love for a singer at the Grand Theatre — who is described in terms that would suit the cataloguing of a figurine — that detains him. But his obsession has warped normal responses. He does not want to be loved for his collection but nor does he want to engage in the chase: "He was tired of pursuing precious objects." He fantasises about one woman but hopelessly misjudges her responses. These animate figurines, it seems, are uncollectable. He turns his attention to gastronomy, but that, too, is a disappointment. "He had come to a depressing conclusion: that luxury is only luxurious under adverse conditions." There is no alternative but to return to Prague because it is a city that suits his melancholic temperament. "A state of tranquil melancholy was all one could aspire to these days!"

And there is the presence of Marta his loyal and devoted servant whom Utz rescued from the ridicule of her village and who adores him in return. They seem to enjoy a fastidiously controlled relationship and once a year go to the country to buy mushrooms. This event occasions a rhapsody from the narrator to the free market: "the business of trade was one of life's most natural and enjoyable pleasures, no more to be abolished than the act of falling in love". But at the same time Utz prefers to stay rather than to join the flow of exiles who sit complaining in rented rooms. "He knew that anti-Communist rhetoric was as deadly as its Communist counterpart." He is disgusted by the complacent self-indulgence of the Western bourgeoisie ("Their menu seemed to consist entirely of desserts") and on crossing the border back to Czechoslovakia notes with relief the absence of advertising billboards, although his seasonal migrations to Vichy would continue. If he sometimes experiences "boredom, verging on fury" with his "lifeless porcelains" he cannot escape them: "The collection held him prisoner." The freedom of Western consumerism has been exchanged for art and its obsessional demands. And while his compatriots attempt to smuggle their valuables out of the country, Utz engages in a trade in the opposite direction.

The narrator continues his dialogue with Utz (while speculating on the nature of his relationship with Marta) and the conversation easily takes off into the higher reaches of fancy:

> 'Chinese porcelain,' he continued, 'was one of those legendary substances, like unicorn horn or alchemical gold, from which men hoped to drink the Fountain of Youth.' (*Utz*, p.103)

The inventor of porcelain, Bottger, had begun as an alchemist and Utz sees alchemy as "a mystical exercise...to find the substance of immortality" rather than a lust for gold. The narrator attempts a mild irony in his description of Utz's porcelain mania and his taking up of alchemical studies, the aim of which is to elevate his mania onto a metaphysical plane "so that if the Communists took the collection, he would nonetheless continue to possess it". Utz's flights of fancy "made me feel quite dizzy" and he tells the narrator how porcelain was regarded in the eighteenth century as the antidote to decay, a concept which underlines the art/creation parallel:

> Things, I reflected, are tougher than people. Things are the change-

less mirror in which we watch ourselves disintegrate. Nothing is more ageing than a collection of works of art... And I realised, as Utz pivoted the figure [of Harlequin] in the candlelight, that I had misjudged him; that he, too, was dancing; that for him, this world of little figures was the real world... And the events of this sombre century — the bombardments, blitzkriegs, putsches, purges — were, so far as he was concerned, so many 'noises off'. (*Utz*, p.113-4)

After Utz's death in March 1974 the narrator returns to Prague, "a city at the end of its tether". He remembers Utz's conviction that history is "always our guide for the future and always full of capricious surprises". With remarkable prescience, or accidental felicity, Chatwin foresees the Velvet Revolution: "in the end, the machinery of repression is more likely to vanish...but with a puff, or the voice of falling leaves". Turning his back on a party of English "dissident watchers" at the hotel who "drank whisky on their credit cards" he goes off in search of Utz's flat to see what happened to the collection. He dines with Orlik who suspects the collection was destroyed and who reveals the truth that Marta and Utz were married in 1952 to forestall eviction by the housing authorities. The plot — which is never the most instrumental element of a Chatwin novel — now suddenly starts to develop at an uncharacteristically brisk pace. Utz, it turns out, had been using his trips to the West to deal in confiscated works of art. Moreover it is his bristly moustache ("without which he might have remained in my imagination, another art collector, of fussy habits and feminine inclinations, whose encounters with women were ambiguous") that is the secret of his sexual appeal to countless "voluminous operatic divas". By applying the stiff bristles of his moustache to the lady's throat "the crescendo of love-making was as ecstatic as the final notes of an aria". The part played in all this by Marta was "a sad one" but after a rebuff in the mid-1960s he is forced to revise his image of himself as the eternal lover and she moves into his bed. "The pink art-silk dressing gown" — which the narrator glimpsed at the time and was disturbed by — "was the emblem of her victory." There is an official marriage in the Prague Spring of 1968.

The narrator's final task is to locate the collection and he bases his quest on the assumption that: "When reconstructing any story, the wilder the chase the more likely it is to yield results."

He accordingly approaches the garbage collectors who were the last people seen in the vicinity of the flat at the time when possible sounds of destruction were heard. He talks to a dust-man/writer who would have emptied the bins and is drawn inexorably to the conclusion that the Utz collection was destroyed because he feels obscurely that it may have been its inevitable fate:

> Or was it a case of iconoclasm? Is there, alongside the tendency to worship images — which Baudelaire called 'my unique, my primitive passion' — a counter-tendency to smash them to bits? Do images, in fact, demand their own destruction? (*Utz*, p.151)

In the end he rejects that hypothesis:

> I believe that in reviewing his life during these final months, he regretted having always played the trickster. He regretted having wheedled himself and the collection out of every tight corner. He had tried to preserve in microcosm the elegance of European court life. But the price was too high. He hated the grovelling and the compromise — and in the end the porcelains disgusted him. (*Utz*, p.152)

His "revised version" of the story is that Utz and Marta, having achieved sexual consummation, "passed their days in passionate adoration of each other, resenting anything that might come between them. And the porcelains were bits of old crockery that simply had to go." Life, in short, triumphed over art. Chatwin was himself to live barely a year longer and this was his last book. He would have known that he was dying when he wrote it and it is impossible for us to read it now without the knowledge that it was the last work of a unique voice that was prematurely silenced. Could he, too, have reason to doubt the consolation, the point, of an art that could not stop the approach of death? The ambiguity in the book — we do not actually know what happened to the collection — is not a structural flaw but a part of its meaning: the lure of art, and our attachment to it, will always be ambiguous. We cannot entirely be sure what its purposes are, or whether the collection is worth keeping.

The critics once again greeted Chatwin's latest book with acclamation. John Lanchester in *The London Review of Books* noted, like most reviewers, that it was written "in Chatwin's leanest and most pared down manner". Noting apparent inconsistencies (Utz, for example, is one moment an exclusive aesthete, next a daring rescuer of Jews from their Nazi persecutors who values a life above a painting) he concludes: "The multiplicity of viewpoints, and the conflicting evidence, generate an uncertainty which is added to by a narrator who is not identified by name, and who may well be Chatwin himself." He saw the book — in comparison with its author's previous works and drawing on a typology of the wide open and the constrained — as a hybrid in that it had "a close focus on one person's life, but at the same time it opens up questions and throws off ideas with cheerful abandon". The novel, he concludes, "gives the reader the sense that Chatwin, like his narrator, is a little bit puzzled by Utz, a little unsure quite how to sum him up." This riddling, faintly indeterminate atmosphere is what gives the book its peculiar flavour. Chatwin is such a strong manipulator of his effects that we are surprised to find him, as it were, off guard, reluctant to sum up.

Peter Conrad in *The Observer* wrote: "Chatwin's work is always about the compulsiveness of ideas and the paper chase on which they lead us through the world; personal relationships (the novel's traditional concern) are secondary to intellectual exploration." He saw *Utz* as ingeniously overcoming this limitation and found it "that punctiliously postmodern thing, a novel about its own problems in getting itself written". He sees "a beautiful analogy" between Utz's collecting and "Chatwin's own frustrated longing to collect Utz himself; to own him like a fictional character, like one of the decorative miniatures, to recreate life as art". Conrad also sees "tantalising" connections with *The Songlines*. The creation myths that underlie the porcelain mania are "middle-European versions of the Aboriginal dream-time". In spite of the formal differences between the two books, the latest one, like its predecessor is "a version of pastoral, a modest myth of the golden age. The timeless space of aboriginal dreaming resembles the illusions of Prague, a labyrinth where you can wander back through history." But, as always, Conrad concludes, "the real excitement derives from an intellectual drama... For Chatwin, ideas are the supreme fictions."

In the *Times Literary Supplement*, Adam Mars-Jones argued that the book "represents perhaps his most sophisticated attempt to reconcile a strong sense of place with a countervailing conviction of displacement, and a temperamental restlessness". He finds the narrative structure "awkward" as a result of the unreliability of the narrator who halfway through the book admits that he has known Utz for only a total of nine hours and who candidly makes things up and contradicts himself with an almost postmodernist indeterminacy. Mars-Jones finds Chatwin's fiction "always a pleasure to read" but has some reservations: "If he has a weakness it is that the insistent detail can seem in some way self-advertising, drawing attention not to the things seen but to the quality of the eye seeing them. If there is a spiritual side to Utz's connoisseurship, after all, there is a material side to Chatwin's, and his sentences can seem like shelves for items of beauty, for fragments of history and culture that have developed beyond mere footnotes, but seem somewhat inert as the ingredients of fiction." He also concludes that the renunciation of art for life (Marta) by Utz at the end of the novel "seems sentimental, after the book's more troubled meditations on the demanding consolations to be found in the perfection of objects".

David Sexton, in *The Spectator*, said of the ending: "This inconclusiveness may have been simply a way of letting go of an unfinished work for Chatwin, but it functions as a spur to the imagination." The book demonstrated, too, "how much a connoisseur Chatwin has remained as a writer...for him travel-writing is itself a way of collecting. His is an acquisitive prose, exhilaratingly capturing things, fixing surfaces. It is not psychological, but intensely visual, almost imagist, setting down appearances with the maximum of objectivity and rhythmic clarity. Adjectives are precise; colours are always given, flowers are named, spatial relations stated." Like Mars-Jones, Sexton is a little wary about this self-assurance which "sometimes verges on the cocksure". The accuracy is like that of the skilled cataloguer: "the mastery too rapid, the detachment too easy". But he concludes that what stops the Chatwin style slipping into manner is "the sense that only the grip of his strong prose secures the writer's relationship to the world outside. It has about it something febrile, obsessive, virtually decadent, and the excitement is catching." More broadly, Sexton sees Chatwin as offering an exemplary response to the dilemma of contemporary fiction writers — the weakening of belief in stories — by creating "a drama of things seen, neither travel-writing nor fiction, a lesson to practitioners of both".

The book was shortlisted soon after publication in September 1988 for the Booker Prize for fiction. It was now clear to the public that Chatwin was very ill indeed and his appearance on television in connection with the prize, against advice from friends, confirmed the full extent of his decline. Many in the literary world knew of his illness and there was a feeling in some quarters that this fact should be acknowledged by the judges, chaired by Michael Foot, and that Chatwin should win. The bookmakers' odds on this annual literary event started to move towards Chatwin but in the end the prize was won by Peter Carey's *Oscar and Lucinda*. He was also pipped at the post for the Whitbread Prize by his friend Salman Rushdie's *The Satanic Verses*.

Less than three months after the Booker ceremony, Chatwin fell into a coma and died of pneumonia in a Nice hospital on the morning of Wednesday 18 January 1989. It was to be some months after his death before the true nature of his illness was acknowledged. In spite of his illness he had been working on a final collection of miscellaneous writing which was published in the spring of 1989 as *What Am I Doing Here* (the question mark unaccountably omitted from what was derived from an exclamation of Rimbaud in Ethiopia). It consisted of the occasional pieces he had written for a variety of magazines, on travel, or art, or personalities. Most of this material has been discussed above but the newer writing in it consisted of some short fictional pieces composed in 1988. These included two short pieces about 'Assunta' a NHS nurse, which reflect his love of the miraculous, and the heartfelt short piece on his father. There are also some short items on the art world which were apparently based on anecdotes familiar to his friends. And there were two 1988 pieces on travel, 'The Albatross', a Chatwin classic involving an overnight dash to Shetland to seek out the black-browed albatross ("I looked at my watch. It was nine o'-clock. I had time to get to King's Cross Station before the night train left for Aberdeen") and 'Chiloe', another beguiling footnote to *In Patagonia*.

The posthumous publication of *What Am I Doing Here*

prompted many reviews that looked back over Chatwin's whole career. Colin Thubron wrote, in *The London Review of Books*, of the mood that the book created in all Chatwin's admirers: "the reader grows haunted by regret for everything Bruce Chatwin would have written had he not died so early". He found the bulk of the pieces to be rich in the qualities that permeate the books: "the obsessive quest for stories, the cool economy of style, the brilliant eidetic gift, the love affair with the bizarre. So they seem like sap at the roots of his books, rather than off-shoots or stray branches". Each essay was "powered by a private passion. Chatwin became fascinated by something or someone, then ran his subject to earth". He was "an omnivore, and loved that hunger in others" and had an unlikely combination of gifts: "His cinematographic sense (he experienced life as a train of images, he once said) was married to its apparent opposite — a questing abstract imagination." Thubron saw Flaubert as a major stylistic influence: that is to say, the scrupulous recording eye of, for example, *Trois Contes*, rather than the less happy influence of the Flaubert of *Salammbo*: "Reviewers taxed him with heartlessness, and sometimes his instinct for pure recording could create a savage divorce between fact and feeling... In Chatwin, the unsparing clarity of vision and his feeling for the cruel and ambivalent were all of a piece. His prose walked a knife-edge."

Chatwin's unbounded enthusiasm was cautiously welcomed by Hilary Mantel in *The Literary Review*: "there is something of the Victorian schoolbook in the broad assertive sweep of his argument about the origins of civilisation" she thought, but noted that he had "nothing of the debunking sensibility. It is as if the notion of pretension — in people, in ideas — has never crossed his mind, and frequently his work is innocent of irony where others would employ it. His tone is optimistic and curious; his prose is without affectation or fakery and is often of a lapidary beauty." Jonathan Keates in *The Independent* noted the lack of malice or resentment in the portraits and concluded: "We have lost one of the few modern writers who could successfully communicate the meaning of joy." Keates also put his finger on the way Chatwin's repeated surprises, as each book appeared, so different from its precursor, "went hand in hand with the power to create a collusion with the individual reader,as though you and he alone knew where the work's real thrust lay".

Perhaps the most interesting of these reviews was that by Hans Magnus Enzensberger in the *Times Literary Supplement*. He asked why, given the contemporary over-production of literature and the "rampant loss of memory" whereby the work of the recently dead was frequently forgotten, the disappearance of Bruce Chatwin should make such a difference. It was not enough, thought Enzensberger, to say that he died young or that he was full of promise. The real "mark of excellence" of Chatwin was his refusal to play the literary game: "Chatwin never delivered the goods that critics or publishers or the reading public expected. Not fearing to disappoint, he surprised us at every turn of the page." His very first book, *In Patagonia*, showed a "sublime disregard for the categories of fiction and non-fiction", nor did it fall for "the illusion of originality". His tales always "admit, and even embrace, the voice of others"; he respected the "experience, mood and the language of other people". The pieces in *What Am I Doing Here* likewise avoided "the pitfalls of the commission" and showed instead "the uncommon spectacle of a writer using the press on his own terms, using the tools and opportunities of journalism to the advantage of literature". Writing as a foreigner, Enzensberger admitted to seeing Chatwin as "the quintessential Englishman" with something old-fashioned in his bearing, although, paradoxically, "about the only prejudice to be found in this writer is his sincere disgust for England". In this he was part of a long line of English refugees from their culture, a phenomenon produced by the imperial past, but he had no trace of the colonial attitude. "For he is not only conversant with other cultures, he goes straight to the heart of what is foreign, much more so than most of his predecessors, from Lawrence to Forster and from Orwell to Lowry." Enzensberger defended Chatwin against the charge of being too baroque or bizarre: "It is not his fault if the world does not conform to the subdued voices and minimal hues of the British landscape...".

It is Chatwin's intellectual pretensions that give Enzensberger his real cause for concern. He accuses Chatwin of a lack of rigour in some of his philosophical and theological speculations and argues that "the laconicism so convincing in his story-tell-

ing will every now and then degenerate into the merely per-
emptory non-sequitur". He is sceptical of Chatwin's suscepti-
bility to that form of ratiocination represented by the Thinker
and the Sage, embodied by such "doubtful figures" as Ernst
Junger or Andre Malraux, and interprets his "theoretical flights
of fancy" as no more than an antidote to "a certain philistine
dread of the intellectual imagination" which is another aspect of
his "flight from Englishness". Enzensberger concludes that
underneath the brilliance of the text:

> There is a haunting presence, something sparse and solitary and
> moving, as in Turgenev's prose. When we return to Bruce Chatwin
> we find much in him that he has left unsaid. (Enzensberger, 1989)

It is the pressure of that "unsaid" that will ensure a permanent interest in Chatwin's writing. In 1992 George Sluizer's film
of *Utz* was released. In spite of being in many ways a handsome
film it makes us understand why Chatwin was indifferent to
filmic treatments and adaptations of his work. So much that
was in the book had to be jettisoned and the director and his
scriptwriter, Hugh Whitemore, removed the final uncertainty
by showing Utz and Marta on the former's deathbed smashing
the collection. The film also inserted an interview with a museum official who tells the American art dealer Marius Fischer,
invented by the film maker to take the place of the narrator, that
Utz had been a dealer in hard currency for the Czech Government, which in the book is no more than a stray hint or suggestion. Sluizer told an interviewer who visited him on the set in
July 1991: "There is a different end to the book. I won't say
what, but let's say in general I do believe in some kind of resolution."

7. THE CHATWIN LEGEND

On Tuesday 6 September 1988, three weeks before the Booker Prize shortlist was announced, a startling headline appeared in the popular newspaper *Today*: TOP AUTHOR CHATWIN FALLS VICTIM TO AIDS. The story was taken up over the next few days by other newspapers, including the *Evening Standard* which reported that these "depressing, though unconfirmed" reports had "cast a shadow over the literary world". Four months later, the same newspaper reported that Chatwin had fallen into a coma and died of pneumonia in a Nice hospital. He had been staying at the home in Grasse of Shirley Conran. The report said that Chatwin's friend and literary executor, the travel writer Redmond O'Hanlon, had confirmed Chatwin had been suffering from Aids for some time. He had received a blood transfusion at a Nice hospital three weeks previously after an earlier one at the Radcliffe Infirmary, Oxford. Chatwin himself had always insisted on an alternative diagnosis. As we have seen, he described his illness as a rare fungus of the bone-marrow picked up in China which ate up, or refused to produce, sufficient red blood corpuscles. The fungus, he explained, had been recorded among ten healthy peasants in Western China, and in the corpuscles of a killer-whale cast up on the shores of Arabia.

This might have seemed more than adequately unprosaic but further inventive variations went into circulation, including the speculation that he had died from eating a thousand year old egg. When the obituaries — mostly written by his friends — appeared in the serious newspapers shortly after his death on 18 January 1989 they referred only to the fungus of the bone marrow as the cause of death. This must have seemed, to those who had read the earlier newspaper accounts, like a deliberate attempt to conceal the facts. Family sources, however, confirm that it was a genuine diagnosis supported by medical opinion (although the reports that Chatwin was also suffering from Aids have never been contradicted). Indeed, in spite of the apparently reliable confirmation of Aids by Redmond O'Hanlon on 8 September 1988, the alternative explanation remained current and one journalist, Sean French, who raised the matter in his column in the *New Statesman and Society*, was bitterly attacked by a fellow journalist, Geoffrey Wheatcroft, in *The Independent Magazine* for what he saw as an unwarranted posthumous 'outing' of Chatwin.

French's argument was that "openness and honesty are among the few weapons that could be of some use in the public campaign against the disease" and that the artist and filmmaker Derek Jarman's public admission that he was HIV positive was by contrast "an act of immense courage and integrity". He went on to note how many travel writers were "of ambiguous sexuality" and concluded that "Chatwin's fictitious disease was another gallant myth, a way of escaping being pinned down to the very end". Although some readers of the magazine reacted angrily to French's piece (one correspondent called it "prurient and mischievous") he insisted that he was right (he alluded to O'Hanlon as a source) and that Aids "has precisely removed the useful freedom certain people had to be ambiguous about just what it was they did do". A more forthright criticism of Chatwin's reticence was published in *The Guardian* nearly a year after his death. Duncan Fallowell, writing on World Aids Day, attacked prominent artists for not being more honest about the disease. "Hypocrisy, lies, distortion, deceit, threats, self-disgust, cooking the facts, and shame — all these," he wrote, "may make life more interesting but they are no good when trying to cope with Aids and all are exemplified in the case of the writer Bruce Chatwin, the most important Aids casualty in the arts to date." Fallowell argued that Chatwin could not admit to having the Aids virus "presumably because it would be tantamount to a confession of the homosexuality to which he was socially maladjusted". At a different level, it would also "make this otherwise very successful man appear to be a loser in life". Fallowell then pressed the argu-

ment further into a terrain that is at once more difficult to be
certain about and more pertinent to Chatwin's readers: the effect of all this on his writing. There is indeed a case for saying
that Chatwin's private life is his own. But if certain knowledge
(and, of course, there is always the possibility that Chatwin did
not have Aids, in spite of the fact that denials of all these press
reports were conspicuous by their absence) becomes available
that has a bearing on writing which exists in the public domain
the case is altered. Fallowell — unlike the present writer — is
confident that we have sufficient knowledge of Chatwin's sexuality for it to be a useful instrument in the interpretation of his
writing. He makes the bold assertion that "his fear of what was
inside him gave his books a shiny enamelled, sterile surface"
and speculated that "Aids and the prowling death gave Chatwin
the opportunity to write an extraordinary book — his character,
which gave us the books we have, meant that he couldn't take
that opportunity". Reading Chatwin's oeuvre in the light of assumptions about his sexuality (taking up stray hints such as
Updike's denotation of the relationship of Benjamin and Lewis
Jones as "a homosexual marriage"; or looking again at the ambiguous sexuality of Dom Francisco da Silva) might eventually
become a critical line of inquiry that will deliver results. The
judicious reader, however, will probably wait for further biographical evidence before striking out in that direction.

But is the reader likely to get it? Fallowell attacked the prominent liberal intellectuals who falsified their public obsequies but
in July 1991 a further front opened up in the war against the
protectors of Chatwin's reputation when the critic David Sexton
took the unprecedented step of firing a shot across the bows of
Chatwin's prospective official biographer, Nicholas Shakespeare. Writing in the *Evening Standard*, Sexton said bluntly that
he doubted whether the track record of this particular biographer gave any confidence that the Chatwin mystique would
be unravelled by him. Rarely can a biographer have been so
publicly warned, long before he has even put pen to paper, to
adopt a more critical approach to the evidence about his subject.
Quoting some fanciful passages from Shakespeare's journalism
about Chatwin, Sexton observed balefully: "These are not the
tones of a realist, let alone a muckraker." For Sexton, Dr
Johnson's biographical standard of "the stability of truth" was a

more reliable touchstone for the recorder of a life than vivid tall stories. "In the memoirs and biographies which are to come," he warned, "Chatwin should not be denied it."

In spite of Sexton's scepticism, however, raw material for the Chatwin legend continued to be mined after his death. There was, for instance, the case of the secret diaries. This story emerged in July 1991 when Redmond O'Hanlon announced the existence of an intimate diary written in code and deposited with the antiquarian bookseller Bertram Rota in London. In spite of a prompt and vigorous denial by Chatwin's widow Elizabeth — who said that her husband never kept diaries and that the notebooks were not dated and were not written in code " though his handwriting was pretty illegible" — O'Hanlon insisted that someone had been employed to decipher the diaries and, keeping the pot of intrigue on the boil, refused to name the putative code-breaker. A close friend of Chatwin's was quoted in *The Times* as saying the diaries gave detailed records of "every personal relationship, and are very explicit about his liaisons". Chatwin's will gave strict instructions that his papers were to be deposited in the Bodleian Library at Oxford and were not to be made available for twenty years after his death but O'Hanlon told *The Times* that he believed they should be published as soon as possible. His fellow literary executor, Susannah Clapp, said she knew nothing about the diaries. Sexton also reported that Chatwin had told O'Hanlon that "he wanted young men to know that he had died of Aids" and that when he had first learned the truth he had entertained ideas of suicide, telling his friend: "I went to Geneva — there's a ravishing place in the Alps that haunts me, a ravishing cliff near Jungfrau — and I wanted to jump off it, or failing that, I thought I'd go to Niger and simply take off my clothes, put on my loincloth, walk out into the desert and let the sun bleach me away." In prosaic fact, he checked into the Radcliffe Infirmary and went on to write *Utz*.

According to Chatwin's friends he was a potent collector and weaver of myths, obsessed with stories, the bizarre, brilliant inventions. Sexton quotes Chatwin's friend, John Ryle: "He was a mythomane, in the best sense of the term. Other people collude in this because it makes their lives more fun. They have no interest in demythologising. When you demythologise, what's

left?" Chatwin's readers might have an answer: six outstand-
ingly original books, products of a talent that can stand effortlessly on its own without the aid of what could all too easily
become a Chatwin industry of literary gossip and second-rate
mythologising, building a legend of the fabulous traveller and
storyteller. Bruce Chatwin wrote and was published in the culture which manufactured Lawrence of Arabia. Anything is
possible.

* * *

Like any richly talented personality, Bruce Chatwin was a complex blend of contrasts. He preached austerity and the frugal
life, urging it as the future of the human race, yet at his death
newspaper reports valued his estate at half a million pounds.
He scorned possessions yet two months before he died Oxfordshire CID was frantically trying to trace a $75,000 sculpture
bought in New York which had gone missing. He seemed to
know everyone of consequence in literary London and in-
habited what Colin Thubron called "a cultural *haute monde*" yet
he loved the wilderness of deserts and the nomadic life. "My
whole life has been a search for the miraculous," he once wrote,
"yet at the first faint flavour of the uncanny, I tend to turn
rational and scientific." He was a product of a very conventional English middle class professional and public school background whose highest praise for the travel writer Robert Byron
was that he was "a gentleman" yet he had difficulties with his
Englishness, telling an interviewer "being an Englishman
makes me uneasy". He sometimes seemed to lean, impercep-
tibly, to the political left, loathing Mrs Thatcher ("her pearls and
prurient lips") yet equally antagonistic towards the hippies and
political activists of the sixties with whom he collided on his
travels. He wanted the world to change but was hypnotised by
traditional ways of living. He called the travel book a
"meaningless category" and was said by one critic to be "not a
travel writer at all" yet he was one of the most distinguished
writers and innovators in the genre to be found on the travel
writing shelves. He wrote that his God was the god of walkers
yet at the end of his life he embraced the conventional Chris-
tianity of the Greek Orthodox Church.

Of his stylistic gifts there was no doubt. He acknowledged few modern English influences on his writing, apart from Robert Byron and, for instruction in the art of dialogue, Noel Coward. He admired the poets of the First World War and the prose rhythms of the seventeenth century divine Jeremy Taylor. His most readily self-declared influence was Hemingway, the early Hemingway of the stories in *In Our Time*. But he loved the great Russian writers up to the present day and he admired Flaubert, Baudelaire, and Rimbaud. But his style was his own, clear, distinctive, spare, beautifully crafted.

At his death Chatwin was planning, it was said, a big novel on a Russian theme. He had just been captivated by the music of the South African composer Kevin Volans, who was to dedicate his album *Cover Him With Grass* to Chatwin, and who was to collaborate on the score of a musical work which received its premiere at the Lincoln Centre, New York on 26 November 1988 performed by the Kronos Quartet. It was based on the poetry of Rimbaud, called *L'homme aux Semelles de Vent* with a libretto by Chatwin. Even in his last weeks he was buzzing with ideas and was reported to be considering writing about South Africa and also about the way in which societies care for the sick. His friend, Michael Ignatieff, ended his obituary in *The Independent* with a vivid cameo of the irrepressible spirit:

> I shall always think of him in the last autumn of his life, lying on the grass outside his house, wrapped up in blankets, lying on cushions, weak, grey-haired and emaciated, but also incorrigibly stylish in a pair of high-altitude ski sunglasses. He said he had bought them for his next trip to the Himalayas. He lay there and talked in a faint whisper, full of cackles and laughter like some majestic and unrepentant monarch in exile, like one of the fantastic and touching figures of his own fiction, staring up in the bright, blue sky, while the white clouds scudded across his black glasses. (*The Independent*, 19 January 1989)

"Incorrigibly stylish," seems the best epitaph we could accord Bruce Chatwin.

SELECT BIBLIOGRAPHY

Works by Bruce Chatwin

Books

In Patagonia (Cape) 1977
The Viceroy of Ouidah (Cape) 1980
On The Black Hill (Cape) 1982
Patagonia Revisited [with Paul Theroux, illustrated by Kyffin Williams] (Michael Russell, Salisbury) 1985
The Songlines (Cape) 1987
Utz (Cape) 1988
What Am I Doing Here (Cape) 1989

Note: all page references in the text are to Picador paperback editions (1979-90)

Articles and introductions

'The Nomadic Alternative', in *The Animal Style,* by Emma Bunker, Bruce Chatwin, Anne Farkas (Asia Society, New York) 1970.
Introduction to *Lady Lisa Lyon* by Robert Mapplethorpe, (Blond and Briggs) 1983.
'I Always Wanted to Go to Patagonia', *New York Times Book Review*, 2 August 1983, pp 6, 34-36.
Introduction to *Journey to Armenia* by Osip Mandelstam [trans Clarence Brown] (Redstone Press) 1989.
Introduction to *A Visit to Don Otavio* by Sybille Bedford, (Folio Society) 1990.

Interviews

'Bruce Chatwin' [with Melvyn Bragg] *South Bank Show* (London Weekend Television) 7 November 1982.

'An Interview with Bruce Chatwin' [with Michael Ignatieff] *Granta*, 21, Spring 1987, pp.23-37.

'Heard Between the Songlines', [with Michael Davie] *The Observer*, 21 June 1987, p.18.

'Songs of the Earth', [with Lucy Hughes-Hallett] *Evening Standard*, 24 June 1987, p.33.

'Born Under a Wandering Star', [with Colin Thubron] *The Daily Telegraph*, 27 June 1987.

Selected Criticism of Bruce Chatwin

Books

Levi, Peter. *The Light Garden of the Angel King*, (Collins, 1972; revised ed. Penguin Books, 1984).

Miller, Karl. *Doubles*, (OUP,1985) Chapter XX, pp 402-9.

Pilkington, John. *An Englishman in Patagonia*. (Century, 1991).

Pritchett, V.S. *Lasting Impressions*, (Chatto, 1990) pp.42-48

Rushdie, Salman. *Imaginary Homelands*, (Granta Books, 1991) pp.226-231; 232-236; 237-240.

Selected Articles

Anon. 'Nomad into novelist', *The Times*, [obituary notice] 20 January 1989.

Anon. 'Diaries adrift', *The Times*, 6 July 1991.

Anon. 'Chatwin accused of hit and myth'. *The Daily Telegraph*, 6 September 1991.

Bayley, John. 'Writeabout'. Review of TS, *The London Review of Books*, pp.3-5.

Clapp, Susannah. 'What Am I Doing Here?', *The Guardian*, [obituary notice] 19 January 1989.

Clarke, Roger. 'The Man With the Footsoles of Wind', *The Sunday Times*, 26 February, 1989.

Conrad, Peter. '9 hours', Review of Utz, *The Observer*, 25 September 1988, p.43.

Deas, Malcolm. Review of IP, *Times Literary Supplement*, 9 December 1977, p.1444.

Duchene, Anne. Review of OBH, *Times Literary Supplement*, 1 October 1982, p 1063.

Enzensberger, Hans Magnus. Review of WAIDH, *Times Lite rary Supplement*, 16 June 1989, p.657.

Fallowell, Duncan. 'When sex becomes sin', *The Guardian*, 1 December 1989.

Fermor, Patrick Leigh. 'Into the blue', Review of TS, *The Spectator*, 11 July 1987, pp 28-29.

Fermor, Patrick Leigh. 'Bruce Chatwin', *The Spectator*, 18 February 1989, p.19-20.

French, Sean. 'Diary', *New Statesman & Society*, 27 January 1989, p.9; 17 February 1989, p.9.

Gale, Iain. 'Brushes with fiction' on TS, *The Independent*, 4 January 1992.

Greenwell, Bill. Review of OBH, *New Statesman*, 1 Oct 1982.

Hemming, John. Review of VO, *Times Literary Supplement*, 5 December 1980, p.1380.

Hockday, Mary. 'Chatwin in Czechoslovakia', *The Independent*, 20 July 1991, p 28.

Holloway, David. 'Footloose in Patagonia', *The Daily Telegraph*, 20 October 1977.

Hope, Mary. Review of VO, *The Spectator*, 15 November 1980.

Hough, Graham. Review of VO, *The London Review of Books*, 6-19 November 1980, p.20.

Ignatieff, Michael. 'Bruce Chatwin', *The Independent* [obituary notice] 19 January 1989.

King, Francis. Review of OBH, *The Spectator*, 2 October 1982.

Lanchester, John. 'A Pom by the Name of Bruce'. Review of Utz. *The London Review of Books*, 29 September 1988, pp.10-11.

Levi, Peter. 'Bruce Chatwin: a nomad with dash', *The Independent*, 21 January 1989.

Mantel, Hilary. 'To be a nomad'. Review of WAIDH, *Literary Review*, June 1989, pp.33-34.

Mars-Jones, Adam. Review of Utz, *Times Literary Supplement*, 23 September 1988, p.1041.

Martin, Brian. Review of VO, *New Statesman*, 7 November 1980.

Miller, Karl. 'Chatwins'. Review of OBH, *The London Review of Books*, 21 October-3 November 1982, p.15.

Richardson, Maurice. Review of IP, *New Statesman*, 21 October 1977.

Sexton, David. 'Aids and telling stories', *Evening Standard*, 25 July 1991, p.19.

Sexton, David. Review of Utz, *The Spectator*, 8 October 1988.

Shakespeare, Nicholas. 'A Very Curious Man'. *The Daily Tele graph Weekend Magazine*, 5 November 1988, pp.36,38.

Shakespeare, Nicholas. 'Bruce Chatwin', *The Daily Telegraph*, [obituary notice] 19 January 1989.

Steiner, George. *Times Literary Supplement*, 16 May 1975.

Thubron, Colin. 'Chatwin and the Hippopotamus'. Review of WAIDH, *The London Review of Books*, 22 June 1989, p.18.

Thubron, Colin. 'Other cultures'. *Waterstone's New Books*, Winter 1991, pp.52-53.

Updike, John. 'The Jones Boys', *The New Yorker*, 21 March 1983, pp.126-132.

Williams, Hugo. 'Freelance'. On OBH, *Times Literary Supple ment*, 29 November 1991, p.18.

Further Reading

Basho, Matsuo. *The Narrow Road to the Deep North*, trans. No-buyuki Yuasa, (Penguin Books, 1986).

Byron, Robert. *The Road to Oxiana*. (1937).

Darwin, Charles. *The Voyage of the Beagle*. (1839).

Diderot, Denis. *Jacques the Fatalist*, trans Michael Henry (Pen-guin Books, 1986).

Gibbons, Stella. *Cold Comfort Farm*. (1932).

Gould, Rupert T. *Enigmas: another book of unexplained facts*, (1929)

Hemingway, Ernest. *In Our Time*. (1926).

Hudson, W H. *Idle Days in Patagonia*. (1893).

Kilvert, Francis. *Kilvert's Diary, 1870-1879*. ed. William Plomer, (1944)

Pascal, Blaise. *Pensées*, trans A J Krailsheimer, (Penguin Books, 1991).

Po, Li and Tu Fu. *Poems* trans Arthur Cooper (Penguin Books 1973).

Poe, Edgar Allan. *The Narrative of Arthur Gordon Pym of Nan tucket*. (1838; ed. Harold Beaver, Penguin Books, 1975)

Pound, Ezra. *Gaudier-Brzeska: a memoir* (1916)

Prichard, Hesketh. *Through the Heart of Patagonia*, (1902)

Ricks, Christopher. (ed.) *The Poems of Tennyson*. (Longman, 1969) pp.1452-3.

Other Media

Grieve, Andrew. (Director) *On The Black Hill*. British Film In
stitute, 1987.
Herzog, Werner. (Director) *Cobra Verde*. 1988.
Sluizer, George. (Director) *Utz*. 1992.
Volans, Kevin. *Cover Him With Grass: in memoriam Bruce Chat-
win*. Landor Barcelona. CD CTLCD 111.

ACKNOWLEDGEMENTS

Acknowledgements and thanks are due to the following who gave information or advice: Gilly Adams (Made in Wales Theatre Company), Richard Booth, Michael Cannon, Hunter Davies, Ros Fry, Andrew Grieve, Simon Harpur, Mary Lewis, Magnus Linklater, Diana Melly, Nancy and Lydia Powell, Dai Smith, Charles Way, Martin Wilkinson, Francis Wyndham, and Francis Wheen.

I am especially grateful to Elizabeth Chatwin for reading and commenting on the manuscript. Any errors that remain, however, are solely the responsibility of the author.

I also wish to express my gratitude for the helpfulness and courtesy of the staff at Llyfrgell Genedlaethol Cymru (The National Library of Wales), Hereford Library, the Museum of Mankind, the British Film Institute, and Sotheby and Co. London Weekend Television kindly arranged a viewing of The South Bank Show, provided a post-production script and gave permission to quote from it.

Particular gratitude is expressed to the series editor John Powell Ward for his constant encouragement and support.

* * *

The publisher acknowledges the help of Jerry Bauer (front cover photograph) and Jane Bown (portrait of Chatwin).

Series Afterword

The Border country is that region between England and Wales which is upland and lowland, both and neither. Centuries ago kings and barons fought over these Marches without their national allegiance ever being settled. In our own time, referring to his own childhood, that eminent borderman Raymond Williams once said: "We talked of 'The English' who were not us, and 'The Welsh' who were not us." It is beautiful, gentle, intriguing, and often surprising. It displays majestic landscapes, which show a lot, and hide some more. People now walk it, poke into its cathedrals and bookshops, and fly over or hang-glide from its mountains, yet its mystery remains.

In cultural terms the region is as fertile as (in parts) its agriculture and soil. The continued success of the Three Choirs Festival and the growth of the border town of Hay as a centre of the secondhand book trade have both attracted international recognition. The present series of introductory books is offered in the light of such events. Writers as diverse as Mary Webb, Raymond Williams and Wilfred Owen are seen in the special light — perhaps that cloudy, golden twilight so characteristic of the region — of their origin in this area or association with it. There are titles too, though fewer, on musicians and painters. The Gloucestershire composers such as Samuel Sebastian Wesley, and painters like David Jones, bear an imprint of border woods, rivers, villages and hills.

How wide is the border? Two, five or fifteen miles each side of the boundary; it depends on your perspective, on the placing of the nearest towns, on the terrain itself, and on history. In the times of Offa and after, Hereford itself was a frontier town, and Welsh was spoken there even in the nineteenth century. True border folk traditionally did not recognise those from even a few miles away. Today, with greater mobility, the crossing of bound-aries is easier, whether for education, marriage, art or leisure. For myself, who spent some childhood years in Here-

136

fordshire and a decade of middle-age crossing between England and Wales once a week, I can only say that as you approach the border you can feel it. Suddenly you are in that finally elusive terrain, looking from a bare height down on to a plain, or from the lower land up to a gap in the hills, and you want to explore it, maybe not to return.

This elusiveness pertains to the writers and artists too. It is often difficult to decide who is border, to what extent and with what impact on their work. The urbane Elizabeth Barrett Browning, prominent figure in the salons of London and Italy in her time, spent virtually all her life until her late twenties outside Ledbury in Herefordshire, and this fact is being seen by current critics and scholars as of more and more significance. The twent-ieth century 'English pastoral' composers — with names like Parry, Howells, and Vaughan Williams — were nearly all border people. One wonders whether border country is now suddenly found on the English side of the Severn Bridge, and how far even John Milton's *Comus*, famous for its first pro-duction in Ludlow Castle, is in any sense such a work. Then there is the fascinating Uxbridge-born Peggy Eileen Whistler, transposed in the 1930s into Margiad Evans to write her (epi-lepsis-based) visionary novels set near her adored Ross-on-Wye and which today still retain a magical charm. Further north: could Barbara Pym, born and raised in Oswestry, ever remotely be called a border writer? Most people would say that the poet A.E. Housman was far more so, yet he hardly ever visited the county after which his chief book of poems, *A Shropshire Lad*, is named. Further north still: there is the village of Chirk on the boundary itself, where R.S. Thomas had his first curacy; there is Gladstone's Hawarden library, just outside Chester and actually into Clwyd in Wales itself; there is intriguingly the Wirral town of Birkenhead, where Wilfred Owen spent his adolescence and where his fellow war poet the Welsh Eisteddfod winner Hedd Wyn was awarded his Chair — posthumously.

On the Welsh side the names are different. The mystic Anne Griffiths; the metaphysical poet Henry Vaughan; the astonishing nineteenth century symbolist Arthur Machen (in Linda Dowling's phrase "Pater's prose as registered by Wilde"); and the remarkable Thomas Olivers of Gregynog, associated with the writing of the well-known hymn 'Lo he comes with clouds descending'. Those descending clouds...; in the border country the scene hangs overhead, and it is easy to indulge in unwarranted speculation. Most significant perhaps is the difference to the two peoples on either side. From England, the border meant the enticement of emptiness, a strange unpopulated land, going up and up into the hills. From Wales, the border meant the road to London, to the university, or to employment, whether by droving sheep, or later to the industries of Birmingham and Liverpool. It also meant the enemy, since borders and boundaries are necessarily political. Much is shared, yet different languages are spoken, in more than one sense.

With certain notable exceptions, the books in this series are short introductory studies of one person's work or some aspect of it. There are no footnotes or indexes. The bibliography lists the main sources referred to in the text, and sometimes others, for anyone who would like to pursue the topic further. The authors reflect the diversity of their subjects. They are specialists or academics; critics or biographers; poets or musicians themselves; or ordinary people with however an established reputation of writing imaginatively and directly about what moves them. They are of various ages, both sexes, Welsh and English, border people themselves or from further afield.

To those who explore the matter further, the subjects — the writers, painters and composers written about — seem increasingly to be united by a particular kind of vision. This holds good however diverse they are in other, main ways; and of course they are diverse indeed. One might scarcely associate, it would seem, Raymond Williams with Samuel Sebastian Wesley, or Dennis Potter with Thomas Traherne. But one has to be careful in such assumptions. The epigraph to Bruce Chatwin's twentieth century novel *On The Black Hill* is a pasage from the seventeenth century mystic writer Jeremy Taylor. Thomas Traherne himself is subject of a recent American study which puts Traherne's writings into dialogue with the European philosopher-critics Martin Heidegger, Jacques Derrida and Jacques Lacan. And a current bestselling writer of thrillers, Ellis Peters, sets her stories in a Shrewsbury of the late mediaeval church with a cunning quiet monk as her ever-engaging sleuth.

The vision (name incidentally of the farmhouse in Chatwin's

novel) is something to do with the curious border light already mentioned. To avoid getting sentimental and mystic here — though border writers have been both — one might suggest lit-erally that this effect is meteorological. Maybe the sun's rays are refracted through skeins of dew or mist that hit the stark mountains and low hills at curious ascertainable angles, with prismatic results. Not that rainbows are the point in our area: it is more the contrasts of gold, green and grey. Some writers never mention it. They don't have to. But all the artists of the region see it, are affected by it, and transpose their highly differ-ent emanations of reality through its transparencies. Mean-while, on the ground, the tourist attractions draw squads from diverse cultural and ethnic origins; agriculture enters the genetic engineering age; New Age travellers are welcome and unwelcome; and the motorway runs up parallel past all — 'Lord of the M5', as the poet Geoffrey Hill has dubbed the Saxon king Offa, he of the dyke which bisects the region where it can still be identified. The region has its uniqueness, then, and a statistically above-average number of writers and artists (we have identified over fifty clear candidates so far) have drawn something from it, which it is the business of the present series to elucidate.

John Powell Ward

The Author:

Nicholas Murray is a freelance writer and journalist living in the Radnor Valley in the Welsh Borders. Born and educated in Liverpool, his poems, articles and reviews have appeared in a wide range of magazines including *The London Review of Books, The Times Literary Supplement, Literary Review, Poetry Review, New Statesman, New Society, Tribune, The Guardian* and *The Independent*.